THE
CAVEMAN
MYSTIQUE

THE
CAVEMAN
MYSTIQUE

Pop-Darwinism and the Debates Over Sex, Violence, and Science

MARTHA McCAUGHEY

Routledge
Taylor & Francis Group
New York   London

Routledge
Taylor & Francis Group
270 Madison Avenue
New York, NY 10016

Routledge
Taylor & Francis Group
2 Park Square
Milton Park, Abingdon
Oxon OX14 4RN

© 2008 by Taylor & Francis Group, LLC
Routledge is an imprint of Taylor & Francis Group, an Informa business

Printed in the United States of America on acid-free paper
10 9 8 7 6 5 4 3 2 1

International Standard Book Number-13: 978-0-415-93475-6 (Softcover) 978-0-415-93474-9 (Hardcover)

Library of Congress Cataloging-in-Publication Data

McCaughey, Martha, 1966-
   The Caveman mystique : pop-Darwinism and the debates over sex, violence, and science / by Martha McCaughey.
      p. cm.
   ISBN 978-0-415-93475-6 (pbk.) -- ISBN 978-0-415-93474-9 (cloth)
   1. Sex role. 2. Men--Psychology. 3. Masculinity. 4. Sex. 5. Homosexuality. 6. Violence. 7. Evolution (Biology) I. Title.

HQ1075.M4 2007
306.7--dc22   2007010352

Visit the Taylor & Francis Web site at
http://www.taylorandfrancis.com

and the Routledge Web site at
http://www.routledge.com

CONTENTS

ACKNOWLEDGMENTS

Many people helped me in many ways over the years during which my thinking, and this book, have taken shape. Years before I knew I'd write this book, I enjoyed both encouragement and superlative instruction in evolutionary theory from Professors Richard Alexander, Donald Brown, David Buss, Barbara Smuts, and Donald Symons at Michigan and UC Santa Barbara.

Once I decided to write this book, the following colleagues, friends, and family members shared readings, offered ideas, and read chapters, sustaining me through the many stages of the project: Eric Ackerman, Mike Ayers, Mary Blaisdell, Megan Boler, Todd Cherry, Adam Dreyfus, Christina French, Wyatt Galusky, Kim Hall, Bernice Hausman, Mike Hudson, Jeremy Hunsinger, Brent Jesiek, Mike Kidner, Katie King, Neal King, Piyush Mathur, Barbara McCaughey, Richard McCaughey, Adam Monroe, Jammie Price, Marc Pyko, Colin Ramsey, Mark Russell, Chuck Smith, Daniel Umlauf, Amber Vellenga, and Christine Watkins. Thanks also go to P. S. Polanah, whose enthusiastic support for all my projects should have been acknowledged sooner. Thanks especially go to Richard Widick, who for many years and across many miles has made himself available to educate and encourage me; without knowing it, he has served as my academic and personal lifeline. In addition, the graduate students in science and technology studies at Virginia Tech were not only intellectually stimulating, but also incredibly good humored. Paul Robertson performed eleventh-hour reformatting and made valuable suggestions on the penultimate draft.

I want to thank the people who helped me with research at various stages of the project: Janet Arnado, Donna Augustine, Dironna Moore, Mark Russell, Donna Trainum, and Daniel Umlauf. I received valuable assistance from the people in the Darwin Collection of the UC Santa Barbara library and in the American Philosophical Society Library in Philadelphia.

I'm grateful to Jeff Hood for permitting me to reprint some of the images (drawn by Jack Lindstrom) from his book *The Silverback Gorilla Syndrome*. Cafepress.com kindly agreed to let me use images of some of their products. Anna Rachel Terman was nice enough to scan and format the digital images for me. Parts of chapter 2 were published previously in *Science As Culture*. Parts of chapters 1 and 4 were published previously in *GLQ* and are used here with the permission of Duke University Press.

"WELCOME BACK TO THE CAVEMAN TIMES":
AN INTRODUCTION

If you were stranded on a deserted island with a woman, would you rape her? This dilemma was put forward by a male scholar attending the second annual conference of the Human Behavior and Evolution Society. I attended this conference, which was held in 1989 at Northwestern University. We were in a session on morality and evolution, and a lively discussion of that dilemma took place for the remainder of the session. I wondered if I was the only woman in the room uncomfortable with the question, with the way the male scholars talked only to one another as men, and with the presumptuousness that raping a woman is a man's choice. Of course, they meant to ask whether it is a choice in the evolutionary sense—whether an innate drive to reproduce would cause an otherwise conscientious, law-abiding man to commit a felony. But what got me was the gall of these male scholars to assume that they *could* rape if they wanted to or were driven to. This astonished me, as did their understanding of the human female as the passive object of the aggressive behaviors men have presumably evolved to dish out. I have been paying attention to claims about evolution, sex, and aggression ever since.

Such claims turn on a trendy story of the caveman. You can find references to man's evolutionary heritage not only in new science textbooks, but also in pop psychology books on relationships, *Playboy* magazine, and Broadway shows. There are caveman fitness plans and caveman diets. *Saturday Night Live*'s hilarious "Unfrozen Caveman Lawyer" and the

1

affronted caveman of the Geico car insurance ads joke about the ubiquity of caveman narratives.

More disturbingly, the Darwinian discourse also crops up when men need an excuse for antisocial behavior. One man, who was caught on amateur video participating in New York City's Central Park group sexual assaults in the summer of 2000, can be heard on video telling his sobbing victim, "Welcome back to the caveman times." How does a man come to think of himself as a caveman when he attacks a woman? What has made so many American men decide that it's the DNA, rather than the devil, that makes them do it?

Everywhere we look we can find accounts of an increasingly fashionable academic exercise: the application of evolutionary theory to human male behavior—particularly deplorable behavior, such as rape, sexual harassment, and aggression, more generally. The evolutionary idea is that our human male ancestors were in constant competition with one another for sexual access to fertile women. The legacy of this "sperm war," we are told, is the unique boorishness of the hairier sex: He is sexually promiscuous; he places an enormous emphasis on women's youth and beauty, which he ogles every chance he gets; he either cheats on his wife or wants to; and he can be sexually aggressive to the point of criminality.[1]

The Caveman Mystique examines evolutionary stories as explanatory narratives of men's sexual desires and behaviors, situated in a broader context of the contemporary gender politics of scientific knowledge. As such this book asks the following questions: How is evolutionary theory presented to men as a science, and scientific ethos, of male sexuality? What social forces today make the caveman identity so tempting? How do men use the mythology of the caveman to experience and explain their own or other men's sexual desires? When we trace this caveman narrative through American culture, what do we learn about the culture itself?

That an evolutionary account of heterosexual male desire has captured the popular imagination is obvious from *Time* magazine's cover story on infidelity, offering an evolutionary explanation for men's philandering ways.[2] *Muscle and Fitness* magazine features an article "Man the Visual Animal" and uses a theory of the evolved difference between human male and female sexual psychologies developed by leading evolutionary psychologist Donald Symons to explain why men leer at women. Under the subheading "Evolution Happens," the author explains,

Not much has changed in human sexuality since the Pleistocene. In his landmark book *The Evolution of Human Sexuality* (Oxford University Press, 1979), Symons hypothesizes that the male's sexual response to visual cues has been so rewarded by evolution that it's become innate.

Such stories provide a means by which heterosexual male readers can experience their sexuality as acultural, primal: "The desire to ogle is your biological destiny."[3]

Evolution may happen (or may have happened), but these stories do not just happen. Their appeal seems to lie precisely in the sense of security provided by the imagined inevitability of heterosexual manhood. In a marketplace of masculine identities, the caveman ethos is served up as Viagra for the masculine soul. As I discuss in chapter 1, just as the 1950s women suffering what Betty Friedan famously called the feminine mystique were supposed to seek satisfaction in their Tupperware collections and their feminine figures, men today have been offered a way to think of their masculinity as powerful, productive, even aggressive—in a new economic and political climate where real opportunities to be rewarded for such traits have slipped away.[4]

In September 1999, *Men's Health* magazine featured a caveman fitness program. Readers are shown an exercise routine that corresponds to the physical movements their ancestors would have engaged in: throwing a spear, hauling an animal carcass, honing a stone. A nice-looking, clean-shaven young man is shown exercising, his physical posture mirrored by a scruffy, animal pelt-clad caveman behind him in the photo. Each day of the weeklong routine is labeled according to the caveman mystique: building the cave home, the hunt, the chase, the kill, the long trek home, preparing for the feast, and rest. It's fitting that the seventh day is one of rest; as I show in chapter 2, evolutionary theorizing has long mirrored a Judeo–Christian ethos. That an exercise plan is modeled after man as caveman reveals the common assumption that being a caveman is good for a man, a healthy existence.

Another issue of *Men's Health* magazine explains "the sex science facts" to male readers interested in "the biology of attraction." We follow the steps of a mating dance, but don't quite understand that's what we're doing. Indeed, we must learn the evolutionary history of sex to see why men feel the way they do when they notice a beautiful woman walking down the street:

Of course, out there in the street, you have no thoughts about genetic compatibility or childbearing. Probably the farthest thing from your mind is having a child with that beautiful woman. But that doesn't matter: what you think counts for almost nothing. In the environment that crafted your brain and body, an environment in which you might be dead within minutes of spotting this beauty, the only thing that counted was that your clever neocortex—your seat of higher reason—be turned off so that you could quickly select a suitable mate, impregnate her, and succeed in passing on your genes to the next generation.[5]

The article proceeds to identify the signals of fertility that attract men: youth, beauty, big breasts, and a small waistline. Focusing on the desire for youth in women, the article tells men that

the reason men of any age continue to like young girls is that we were designed to get them pregnant and dominate their fertile years by keeping them that way.... When your first wife has lost the overt signals of reproductive viability, you desire a younger woman who still has them all.[6]

And, of course, male readers are reminded that "your genes don't care about your wife or girlfriend or what the neighbors will say."[7]

Amy Alkon's *Winston-Salem Journal* advice column, "The Advice Goddess," uses an evolutionary theory of men's innate loutishness to comfort poor "Feeling Cheated On," who sent a letter complaining that her boyfriend fantasizes about other women during their lovemaking. The Advice Goddess cites a study by Bruce J. Ellis and Donald Symons (whose work is also mentioned in *Muscle and Fitness*) to conclude that "male sexuality is all about variety. Men are hard-wired to want you, the entire girls' dorm next door, and the entire girls' dorm next to that."[8]

It's not just these popular or humorous accounts of men and women that are based in some version of evolutionary theory. Even serious academic arguments rely on evolutionary theories of human behavior. For example, Steven Rhoads, a member of the University of Virginia faculty in public policy, has written *Taking Sex Differences Seriously* (2004), a book telling us why gender equity in the home and the workplace is a feminist pipedream. Rhoads argues that women are wrong to expect men to take better care of children, do more housework, and make a place for them as equals at work because, he states, "men and women still have different natures and, generally speaking, different preferences, talents and interests."[9] He substantiates much of his argument about the divergent psychological predispositions in men and women with countless references to studies done by evolutionary scholars.

The familiar portrayals of sex differences based in evolution popularize and legitimize an academic version of evolutionary thought known increasingly as evolutionary psychology, a field referred to as the "science of the mind."[10] Since the late 1980s, increasing numbers of college courses and textbooks have taught the significance of evolution by natural selection for understanding patterns of human behavior. Many people have heard of Edward O. Wilson's work and the term he coined—*sociobiology*—that applies to a broader scope of inquiry, namely the application of evolutionary theory to the study of humans and animals. Others may have heard of the fields of Darwinian anthropology, evolutionary biology, evolutionary human behavior, or evolutionary psychology.[11] Contributors to the volume *The Sociobiological Imagination* span eighteen such fields or subfields.[12] While these areas have a variety of methodological approaches and scholarly bases for the application of evolutionary theory to human behavior, I label all this scholarship human behavior and evolution (HBE), after the name of the American academic association in which they've come together since 1988—the Human Behavior and Evolution Society.[13]

HBE has become an academic institution. Entire college curricula now exist: students can take courses in human behavior and evolution and can pursue graduate study in the specialty. In addition, both a professional society and a journal devoted to the study of human behavior from an evolutionary perspective give the field a professional identity. HBE scholars have for more than two decades been writing books, from *The Evolution of Human Sexuality* to *The Evolution of Desire* to *Sperm Wars*, seeking to establish the importance of evolutionary theory in explaining human behavior—particularly male sexual behavior. The combination of the scholarly and popular attention to evolution and human male sexuality has increasingly lodged American manhood in an evolutionary logic.

It's a daunting task to write a book on the increasingly potent scientific claims about human male sexuality made since the late 1980s by contemporary evolutionary theorists and their enthusiasts. Most general readers seem far more eager to learn about how evolution makes us behave than to consider what kind of difference evolutionary thinking has made to contemporary consciousness. Put differently, it seems far more fun to read about who you are than to challenge the certainty of that self-understanding.

I wouldn't blame evolutionary scientists if at first glance they assumed this book was yet another feminist rant accusing them of being sexist pigs peddling the latest form of social Darwinism. In contrast, feminists might as easily jump to the conclusion that I'm defending evolutionary scholarship or making biologically determinist claims about men's behavior. And moreover, the average American guy might assume that I'll pay no attention to his emotional and economic struggles. Still others might imagine that I, as a feminist who seeks a world of gender justice, want to use evolutionary claims about men's putatively natural inclinations to ogle, harass, and rape women as justification for criticizing or controlling men.

So, realizing that I'm walking into an academic and a political minefield, let me state what this book is *not* attempting to do. I do not provide a review of HBE scholarship about men, refuting each claim or theory in the field, nor do I seek to persuade anyone about the "real" nature of men. Instead, I examine sociologically the ideas and frames of reference that most people take for granted. This reflexivity is a hallmark of the "sociological imagination." This book is not the leftist or feminist equivalent of evolutionary theorizing, which has come to be called the "sociobiological imagination." It's not really the nurture side of the old nature/nurture debate. Instead, I investigate how men come to know what they know about themselves.

This suggests that evolution is an ideology—which is not to suggest that humans got here via God's creation or some means other than evolution by natural selection. Not being a religious person myself, I almost forgot to anticipate that some people, being wedded to the notion of creation over that of evolution, might try to read this book for a position on that divide. ("What? She says evolution is an ideology? She must be a Creationist!) I am, in fact, a Darwinist, but I want to interrogate some applications of the theory of evolution by natural selection. I pay particular attention to the ways evolution has circulated in the past 15 to 20 years as an ideology.

Positioning evolutionary arguments about human nature as an ideology is to understand that people think and act in ways that take evolutionary theory, however they construe it, as a self-evident truth. Furthermore, positioning evolutionary theory applied to humans as an ideology allows us to examine the way evolutionary ideas about male sexuality circulate in our culture. To put it more directly, it allows us to interrogate the way some people come to make certain claims about men and gives us a sense of how men might come to feel like cavemen. Treating scientific arguments as discourses—cultural narratives that function to produce what they intend to describe as *a priori*—reveals that the discourses of HBE theory are political. They are the supporting cultural structures of the hegemonic ideology that shapes a variety of sexual practices. *The Caveman Mystique* thus challenges the convenient innocence with which men invoke science to explain their bodies and their actions by putting those narratives in cultural and historical perspective.

Of course, my study does not presume that *all* guys think they're cavemen—only that enough do to make it worth investigating. Nor does it test or prove the effect of Darwinian discourse; it assumes that popularity translates into widespread influence, given the popular expressions of caveman sentiment.[14] The range and character of the truth effect of HBE thought—what historian of ideas Michel Foucault might have called an emergent *biopolitical regime*—can be intimated by considering how the participants in the conference discussion of the island rape scenario might behave if, having concluded at their conference that men would be driven to rape their unfortunate island cohabitant, and if they actually were marooned under those conditions on their flight home, their freshly gained knowledge of natural male rape behavior would inevitably factor into their behavioral self-monitoring.[15] As feminist philosopher Judith Butler argues in *Bodies that Matter*, there is no naming of a thing that is not a further shaping of it.[16] In naming the evolutionary foundations of male sexual behaviors, evolutionary theorizing about such behaviors does more than just describe an inert field of objects (though its language tends to produce just such an image among its audiences), it shapes male sexual behavior and identity.

The Caveman Mystique explores the many ways in which the discourse of HBE becomes part of popular consciousness, a sort of cultural consensus about who men are. This type of analysis follows the logic of French theorist Roland Barthes, who in his book *Mythologies* explains that influential cultural myths work as taken-for-granted systems of meaning—particularly when people don't understand the historical conditions that gave rise to those myths.[17] Without a critical, historical view of how scientific stories emerged to answer questions about men's sexual behaviors and feelings, evolution has become the paradigm through which many people understand men.

Several books offer important critiques of evolutionary discourse. Sarah Blaffer Hrdy's *Mother Nature* combines her expertise as both a feminist and evolutionary theorist to critique the sexism in, and improve, evolutionary theory about women.[18] Marlene Zuk, another feminist evolutionary biologist interested in animal behavior, has written *Sexual Selections* in order to explain what we can and cannot learn about ourselves from the study of nonhuman animal sexual behavior.[19] Biologist and science studies scholar Elisabeth Lloyd's *The Case of the Female Orgasm* addresses biases in evolutionary theories about the female orgasm.[20] *The Caveman Mystique* differs from these books not only because my focus is on humans rather than animals, and men rather than women, but because my goal is not to set the evolutionary record straight or advance the science of evolutionary theory per se. Instead, I want to analyze the political and moral sway of evolutionary arguments precisely because they have truth effects; they get lived out as real biological truths.

Sociologist Ullica Segerstråle's *Defenders of the Truth* offers a rich history of the sociobiology controversy, including insights based on interviews with key sociobiologists.[21] Segerstråle, however, does not comment on the popularization of sociobiological claims or their connection to men or to embodied masculinity. *The Caveman Mystique* presents a missing piece of the puzzle, one that helps explain not only why sociobiology might have attracted so much attention, but also how such intellectual ideas can become embodied beliefs. In addition, while *Defenders of the Truth* is written in a way apposite its scholarly audience, I write in a way that, I hope, will reach as wide an audience as the pop-Darwinism I examine.

Other scholars have shown the individualistic, capitalistic, sexist, and Judeo–Christian ideological underpinnings of certain evolutionary stories. Feminist scholars and my own discipline of sociology both now invoke evolutionary theory as their academic archrival. The typical sociology or women's studies textbook explains that *our* field views people as social creatures; *theirs* views people as biologically driven. Such a position oversimplifies both fields. It paints evolutionary theorists as biological determinists or conservative reactionaries à la Social Darwinism. Moreover, it reinforces a mind–body dualism in sociology and ignores the concerns about human nature in this discipline's history.[22]

The field of women's and gender studies has increasingly put masculinity into scholarly focus. Many wonderful books, such as Susan Bordo's *The Male Body*, Susan Faludi's *Stiffed*, and Michael Kimmel's *Manhood in America* have critiqued and/or chronicled popular modes of masculinity.[23] These studies commonly emphasize film, television, sports, the military, the economy, and pornography, and overlook the impact of scientific writing—and, specifically, evolutionary theory—on modern masculinity. Five excellent essays in the collection *Constructing Masculinity* concern the social institution of science and its impact on masculinity, race, and sexuality;[24] however, none of these addresses the popular story of the caveman or evolutionary claims about men. The caveman is certainly not the only form of masculine identity in our times. But the emergence of a caveman mystique tells us much about the authority of science, the flow of scientific ideas in our culture, and the embodiment of those ideas.

In *Science, Culture and Society*, Mark Erickson explains the connection between science and society in our times:

> We live with science: science surrounds us, invades our lives, and alters our perspective on the world. We see things from a scientific perspective, in that we use science to help us make sense of the world—regardless of whether or not that is an appropriate thing to do—and to legitimize the picture of the world that results from such investigations.[25]

In a culture so attached to scientific authority and explication, it is worth examining the popular appeal of evolutionary theory and its impact on masculine embodiment. Erickson argues that we must understand society in order to understand science and—as important—understand science in order to understand society. In this same vein, *The Caveman Mystique* suggests that understanding the increasingly popular discourse of evolutionary science sheds light on modern masculinity.

Much scholarship has examined science as culture, but few studies have addressed science as *embodied* culture. Similarly, while much attention has been paid to rape culture and the importance of fighting violence against women—including a focus on the female body—virtually none has been paid to the role played by men's narratives of their bodies in perpetuating violence against women. Approaching scientific knowledge and writing as embodied culture continues the approach I have taken in my earlier work on the importance of ideology to embodiment. My 1997 study of the women's self-defense movement, *Real Knockouts*, argues that rape culture cons us into thinking that men can't help but rape and women can't do much about it, given physical differences in size, strength, and temperament.[26] That book examines the physical expectations associated with the ideology of femininity in our rape culture. I argue that when women learn the aggressive posture of self-defense, they challenge

the embodied ethos of rape culture, and consequently expose femininity as a social fiction that is accepted or challenged at the level of the
body. The flip side of this argument involves the embodiment of manhood, for the embodied ideology of rape culture involves both the myth
of the weak, vulnerable woman as well as her "cave day" counterpart: the
aggressive, unstoppable man. In fact, while I was writing *Real Knockouts*,
people routinely reminded me that scientists had already proven that men
had evolved to be sexual aggressors. Hence, I turn my attention to this
increasingly popular evolutionary narrative.

While many public intellectuals place their scholarship in the middle
of struggles over material inequalities such as homelessness or workplace
discrimination, my project is primarily about knowledge, identities, and
bodies—and the struggle over which knowledges will gain a foothold in
our culture and to what effect. My way of studying how inequality operates is to ask how scientific claims create a story of manhood, and how
individual men may come to incorporate that discourse into an embodied
ethos of evolved manhood. How we think about and act out a gendered
identity influences how we frame our behavior and evaluate the behavior
of others.

To study evolutionary science as culture, *The Caveman Mystique* follows
the particular narrative of evolved manhood as it gets told and invoked in
popular culture, situated in the context of the widening impact of professional biological knowledge. Dorothy Nelkin and M. Susan Lindee's *DNA
Mystique* shows how the discourse of the gene has proliferated throughout
popular culture, from discussions of Elvis Presley's genes to those of DNA
as the secular equivalent of the Christian soul.[27] In a similar way, *The Caveman Mystique* traces the popular emergence of an evolutionary discourse of
male sexuality. I argue that ideas about evolution's effect on male sexuality
are linked in scientific texts, TV shows, popular men's magazines, public
performances, and other cultural forms. In his work on television as culture, John Fiske argues that such discourses form "a crucial part of the
social dynamics by which the social structure maintains itself in a constant
process of production and reproduction: meanings, popular pleasures, and
their circulation are therefore part and parcel of this social structure."[28]

Such an analysis employs a methodology known as *intertextuality*.[29] I
show linkages among scientific and popular texts about men's evolutionary
heritage by suggesting that a code runs through all of these texts, and that
these texts can be understood as genres of knowledge generation. Fiske

calls codes "the agents of intertextuality through which texts interrelate in a network of meanings that constitutes our cultural world."[30] From these cultural codes we can see ways of thinking, ideologies, and symbolic logics that frame male bodies in relation to a cultural sex/gender system. Looking at these textual codes is a route to a significant form of social analysis. And it exposes these texts as social forces in their own right.[31]

Those evolutionary theorists who have heard my argument have told me that they object to my bringing up, on the one hand, what the reputable evolutionary psychologist David Buss says, together with, on the other hand, *Men's Health* and *Men's Fitness* magazines. Arguing that they can't control what popular magazines do with their scientific ideas, they see me as an irresponsible researcher for examining the scientific arguments together with their popular versions (or distortions). They resent the way I seem to add my politics to their scientific work.

But these scientists and the knowledge they produce are involved in both popular culture and politics in at least four ways. First, popular debates drive the overall research questions in HBE: Why do men rape? Why are women complaining about how they're treated in the workplace? Why do men desire big-breasted women and pornography? And so forth. Second, popular culture influences scientists' assumptions about gender and sexuality. Third, scientific claims have popular, social consequences. Finally, distinctions between professional and popular evolutionary theory blur in many ways. In order to understand the interplay between professional scientific and popular understandings of evolution and male sexuality, we must examine the discourse of men's evolved sexuality through a variety of cultural texts.

Some senior scholars in the HBE field intentionally write books for popular audiences, such as E. O. Wilson's *On Human Nature* and Richard Dawkins's *Selfish Gene*.[32] Wilson's later book *Consilience* was promoted via a magazine-article version, "The Evolution of Morality," which made the cover of *Atlantic Monthly*.[33] Alfred Russel Wallace, a professional scientist and contemporary of Darwin, wrote most of the time commercially, for the public. Contemporary MIT psychology professor Steven Pinker has written witty books for a wide audience, including comic strips and allusions to writers from Woody Allen to Emily Dickinson, to show that humans have a nature based in evolutionary pressures for reproductive success. Zoologist Robin Baker's *Sperm Wars* is a citation-free, trade-press version of an earlier academic book, *Human Sperm Competition*, and has now been translated into twenty different languages.[34] Zoologist Desmond Morris's television special *The Human Animal* shares with a wide audience his ideas about evolution's impact on human mating preferences.[35] HBE theorists' appearances on television for interviews further indicate a willingness to help communicate their work to a wide audience.

It would be a mistake, then, to ignore the interplay between science and popular culture and for scientists to claim that the flow of evolutionary ideas in our culture has nothing to do with them. In *The Descent of Darwin*, a study of the popularization of Darwinism in Germany between 1860 and 1914, historian Alfred Kelly explains that a handful of thinkers (for example, Charles Darwin, Albert Einstein, Sigmund Freud, Karl Marx, Isaac Newton, and Friedrich Nietzsche) are the source of many widely held ideas, and that the paths these ideas took into the minds of millions remain largely uncharted. While those great ideas were often popularized in watered down and distorted ways, their proliferation is no less worth studying. As Kelly puts it,

> Never mind that no seminal thinker ever said without qualification that, say, man was a beast or that science could solve all problems. A society in which the majority affirms these beliefs—with varying degrees of sophistication—is nonetheless profoundly different from one in which the majority denies them.[36]

Similarly, Nelkin and Lindee's *DNA Mystique* traces the discourse of DNA through popular culture not because popular DNA stories are scientifically accurate, but because they reveal common beliefs, filter complex ideas, reflect cultural values, and create a framework for people's expectations.[37]

Scientific texts can be interpreted by readers, magazine writers, and students in multiple ways. The meaning and consequences of scientific theory are not confined to a scientist's words or intentions. Rather, the meaning of evolutionary stories depends on other cultural texts that make sense of male sexuality. Scientific stories about evolution and manhood have no simple meaning; rather, they are intertextual—that is, meaningful in a context of other stories about manhood, nature, and science, part of "a network of textual relations."[38] *The Caveman Mystique* argues that the evolutionary stories generated by scientists become part of popular knowledge and inform social experience, producing a popular embodied ethos of manhood. This book thus follows a discourse on aggressive male heterosexuality through various texts, popular as well as academic. By examining the way these texts are linked, I highlight the representational context of evolutionary narratives and show how a man's consciousness might be linked to that representational context.

Consequently, *The Caveman Mystique* addresses three wider debates about knowledge, politics, and gender, which I discuss in chapter 1: (1) the *sperm wars*, or the increasingly popular evolutionary theory of competitive, aggressive male sexuality; (2) the *sex wars*, or the feminist debates over what kind of sexual agents women can and should be compared to men; and (3) the *science wars*, or the debates over the place of politics and inter-disciplinary critique in science. My project intends to show that humani-ties, social science, feminist, and cultural studies scholars (i.e., the least "sciencey" types) can and should assess the subject matter addressed by scientists. In this project, I take a "translator's position," which I achieved through a series of coincidences that have kept me interested in HBE thought since the 1980s.

I witnessed the development of the academic struggles at the heart of this project from the start of my academic career, as an undergraduate at the University of Michigan. At Michigan in the 1980s, I saw the develop-ment of, and took classes in, the evolution and human behavior program, which reflected the rise of evolutionary theory applied to human behavior and psychology and which in 1988 sponsored a conference that resulted in the formation of the Human Behavior and Evolution Society. My HBE teachers were wonderful and I was fascinated by evolutionary accounts of everything from rape to infanticide to the pleasure we take in music. David Buss gave a memorable presentation on sex differences in mating strategies, research for which he is now widely known.

I also came into feminist consciousness at the height of the femi-nist sex wars, when we debated questions like, "Have we conceived of women as only the passive objects of male sexual desire?" Feminist ques-tions about the battle of the sexes overlapped with the questions addressed by HBE scholars. I did not see evolutionary explanations as threatening to my feminism; indeed, I figured I could commit myself to values and policies for gender justice regardless of which sex differences turned out to be natural. Plus, I figured that our current society hardly resembled the one in which our ancestors had evolved to survive. If today's society gave men an advantage over women (though even this is oversimplified, given race- and class-based inequities that give some women advantages over many men), it hardly meant that life had always been a hunting and sex fest for the human male while nasty, brutish, and short on foreplay for the human female.[39] But *even if* it turned out to be the case that ancestral men really did drag women into caves and rape them, that did not mean that men could not be reformed or controlled and that women could not fight such injustice.

Later, in graduate school at the University of California–Santa Barbara, I continued my study of HBE thought, benefiting from the fine HBE scholars who taught there. I remember reading an advance copy of an article by the influential Leda Cosmides and John Tooby in Don Symons' seminar on human nature. I remained fascinated by the fact that feminist and evolutionary theorists both took an interest in sex and violence, and I gave a presentation on this very issue that began with the sentence, "Both evolutionary and feminist theorists say women are defined in terms of their fuckability." Yes, I was young and impetuous, but this also reveals how comfortable I felt with my HBE professors.

At the same time, UC–Santa Barbara gave me the opportunity to debate what kind of knowledge sociologists and scientists could create in light of poststructuralist critiques of the false separation of knowledge and power. I studied gender and sexuality as the controversial new "queer theory" emerged, immersing myself in arguments that sex categories were social fictions made, as Judith Butler argued in her 1990 landmark book, *Gender Trouble,* to look like natural essences.[40] My peers and I began to reconsider the ways we'd originally figured ourselves for studying "gender"—the social patterns we learn for expressing masculinity and femininity—leaving "sex" to the biologists. We realized instead that sex was gendered, that culture informs our understanding of nature and sexual difference.

Feminist scholarship had gained legitimacy as a source of information about social institutions, identities, and knowledges about gendered bodies. Feminist science studies zeroed in on the role of science in creating supposedly neutral knowledges about female and male bodies. The science wars debated the place of politics in science and the value of cultural studies for critiquing scientific claims. And the increasing emphasis in social and cultural studies on the body as a site of cultural inscription made me interested in how scientific discourses of sexuality and gendered bodies became lived ideologies. Meanwhile, I took part in another, not-so-theoretical debate thundering across college campuses in the late 1980s

and into the early 1990s. Feminist activists brought to public consciousness the problem of date rape, making violence against women one of the
defining issues of third-wave feminism.

My travels in both evolutionary and feminist circles highlighted
for me the interesting congruence between feminist and evolutionary
theories. After all, evolutionary theorists aren't the scholars ignoring or
denying sexist practices like rape and sexual harassment. Nor are they
unsympathetic to women's anger about those practices and the individual
strategies and social movements that have attempted to resist or transform
them. There were times when, as a student, only my professors, who were
either evolutionary theorists or feminists, were willing to talk about such
issues. Of course, it's equally fascinating that these two groups seem to
dislike each other so much and confront social problems so differently. I
ended up teaching in an interdisciplinary program of women's studies, a
field, like HBE, often subject to mischaracterization by people who know
little about the research in it.

My experiences with HBE theorists help me to avoid a crude critique,
which is easy and common for feminists and other leftists to level against
HBE thinking. The statement of the Ann Arbor, Michigan, collective Science for the People, titled *Biology as a Social Weapon* and one of the first
published formal criticisms of sociobiology in the late 1970s, remains typical: "[Sociobiology tells us that] we should accept the world as it is rather
than struggle in vain for peace, women's rights, participatory democracy, or
a more equal distribution of wealth."[41] I never knew about this group while
I lived in Ann Arbor, but I did take a course in evolutionary biology from
Richard Alexander, one of the group's targets at the time. I know that HBE
theorists like Alexander offer their ideas not to enable male revolt against
feminist expectations (and certainly not to encourage sexual aggression);
they want to help people understand human nature and, on that basis, con-
ceive improved practices, create better policies, and promote the peaceful
solutions they believe science promises. In this way, they're scientists with
a moral purpose, scientists "gone philosophical." Their scientific theory is
presented as moral theory. Rape, for example, is a biological "original sin"
that men can overcome. Evolutionary theorists tend to hope that their work
forces men to take moral responsibility, even though it is often popularly
perceived in ways that reduce men's moral agency.

The translator's position I take on the debates over sex, violence, and
science provides insight into the ways scientific ideas get popularized and

embodied. My experiences with evolutionary theorists help me understand, for instance, that they truly believe feminists are living in ivory-tower, idealistic fantasy worlds, fueled perhaps by our own atypical gender-bending lives, female partners, or extrasensitive husbands. Ignoring the harsh reality of our animal natures and denying the biological bases of the problems we've identified, they reason, will prevent us from finding real solutions to them.

Given this, I think I should mention something about my personal life, beyond my familiarity with evolutionary theorists and my being a feminist. In the middle of writing this book, I was struck by the irony of my personal and professional situations. In my late thirties, I had given dozens of conference presentations, published more than enough academic papers, delivered many public speeches, and otherwise focused my attention almost exclusively on my career. It dawned on me that I stood a better chance of making full professor than of having a child. It's not that I hadn't wanted a mate or a child; I'd always pictured myself with both. I envisioned family dinners, warm holidays, shared meaning, planning my future with someone.

However, I could not seem to find a man who wanted much more than a sexual relationship, and so found myself telling a therapist about my desire for true love, a commitment, and a family. The therapist to whom I made this confession said that it is normal for a woman to want a relationship rather than just casual sex. After all, he explained, there are sex differences and those mean that women just don't like casual sex as much as men do. Women, he continued, crave a relationship context when they have sex because for them having sex bears the consequences of gestation, lactation, and other physical burdens of motherhood. Men have their own biological reasons for wanting to inseminate as much as possible with little consequence. But, I protested, I'm an independent career woman of the 21st century, whose casual sexual encounters are protected from consequences by both safe-sex methods and birth control—and who in any case had enough resources to raise a baby alone. So why don't I—of all women—want casual sex with men? He said that my current situation mattered little given what is hardwired in my female brain.

Why would a therapist tell me this? I didn't tell him that my book was about evolutionary explanations of men's sexual behavior in contemporary society. Obviously, his comments indicate the prevalence of evolutionary answers to certain social problems and individual feelings. But it wasn't just that my therapist accepted the dialogue of evolutionary science; my own life seemed to be providing evidence for it. If I were ever disposed to believe evolutionary theories of sex-linked differences in mating, it would be now. Clearly, then, I am hardly one of the liberal academics whose lifestyle prevents me from seeing how men behave out there in the real world.

In fact, my lifestyle allowed me to see the omnipresence of Darwinian discourse. Being single for so long meant that I've dated enough to hear regular guys also invoke these evolutionary stories. On one occasion, a date complimented my "waist-to-hip ratio," a concept directly out of the HBE literature arguing that men are more physically attracted to a female form with physical proportions for breeding.[42] My date—who, I should mention, was not an evolutionary scholar (or a scholar of any kind)— went on to explain that he also liked large breasts, since they are a sign of fertility.

I recognize the lure of this narrative. After all, it provides an explanation for patterns we do see and for how men do feel in contemporary society, tells men that they are beings who are the way they are for a specific reason, offers them an answer about what motivates them, and carries the authority of scientific investigation about their biological makeup. Plus, it's fun: thinking of the reasons you might feel a certain way because such feelings might have been necessary for your ancestors to survive a hostile environment back in the Pleistocene epoch can be a satisfying intellectual exercise.

Still, organizing one's life narrative according to these evolutionary explanations does not make sense to me. First of all, the evolutionary explanation of men's sexual behavior is an all-encompassing narrative enabling men to frame their own thoughts and experiences through it. As such, it's a *grand narrative,* a totalizing theory explaining men's experiences as though all men act and feel the same way, and as though the ideas of Western science provide a universal truth about those actions and feelings.

I'm skeptical of this kind of totalizing narrative about male sexuality because evolution applied to human beings does not offer that sort of truth. The application of evolutionary theory to human behavior is not as straightforwardly scientific as it might seem, even for those of us who believe in the theory of evolution by natural selection. It is a partial, political discourse that authorizes certain prevalent masculine behaviors and a problematic acceptance of those behaviors. I think there are better—

less totalizing, and differently consequential—discourses out there that describe and explain those same behaviors. I'm also skeptical of men's use of the evolutionary narrative because, at its best, it can only create "soft patriarchs"—kinder, gentler cavemen who resist the putative urges of which evolutionary science makes them aware.[43]

My quarrel is not with HBE theorists alone. Darwinian ideas are often spread by HBE enthusiasts—bestselling authors, secondary school teachers, professors outside the HBE field, science editors of various newspapers and magazines, and educational television show producers—who take up evolutionary theorists' ideas and convey them to mass audiences. Evolutionary thinking has become popular in part because it speaks to a publicly recognized predicament of men. As I show in chapter 1, since 1990 the problem of men's violence has been a topic of national discussion. Even President Bill Clinton's 1994 State of the Union address named young men's gun violence as a source of national moral decline.[44] Moreover, changing economic patterns have propelled men's flight from marriage and breadwinning, in conjunction with women's increased independence. If a man today wants multiple partners with as little commitment as possible, evolutionary rhetoric provides an answer as to why.

The theory of evolution wasn't always widely understood as a moral answer about men or any other human value or social issue. In fact, as I explain in chapter 2, the story of evolution was originally seen as a threat to morality and to male–female interactions. A large number of the most "civilized" men in nineteenth-century Europe refused to accept the notion that man descended from apes. In Darwin's day, the theory of evolution was resisted by privileged men because it seemed to imply the breakdown of civility, of moral certainty, and of a divinely inspired heterosexual bond. Back then, sexuality was so exceedingly racialized—not only did nineteenth-century doctors and scientists draw explicit parallels between black people and apes, but they also spoke of the sexuality of non-Western people as animalistic, instinctive, and uncivilized—that privileged white Western men did not want to identify as animals, as cavemen, or as apemen. But since that time evolution has turned into one of the most powerful and consequential theories of human nature and behavior. That today so many men find solace in evolutionary explanations of who they are, in an identity as cavemen, is both ironic and worth investigating.

Chapter 2 traces how and why Darwin's theory has been adapted for use in a way so different from a century ago. The idea that humans have evolved through natural selection has become not only acceptable, but paradigmatic in many areas. Indeed, evolution and its presumed influence on who we are and how we act is a script of contemporary culture, an assumed truth even for those who have never read Darwin or any contemporary evolutionary theorist. Whereas a man a century or two ago would likely have understood his behavior in religious terms, today men commonly understand themselves in evolutionary terms. As this book will show, evolution has become a religion of its own—a source of meaning, inspiration, self-knowledge, and guidance for moral judgments.

Evolution has become not only a grand narrative, but a lived ideology. Maleness and femaleness, like heterosexuality and homosexuality, are not simply identities, but *systems of knowledge*[45] that inform thinking and acting. Chapter 3 explains that popularized Darwinism is now a series of embodied habits—a second nature taken for nature. I use sociologist Pierre Bourdieu's concept of *habitus* to capture the ways in which culture and knowledge—including evolutionary knowledge—implant themselves at the level of the body, becoming a set of attitudes, tastes, perceptions, actions, and reactions. I, therefore, refer to the man embodying evolutionary precepts unreflexively as *Homo habitus*. The status of science as objective, neutral knowledge helps make evolution a lived ideology because it feels truthful, natural, and real.

Studying the interplay between evolutionary scientific discourse and pop culture allows me to show the way heterocentrist evolutionary narratives dominate the cultural landscape and interest the popular press more often than competing theories. But I consider not only popular perversions of Darwinian thought or particular scientists' failures at empirical rigor. In chapter 4, I take HBE theorists to task for not considering alternative evolutionary explanations. I provide a series of resistant readings of our evolutionary past to show that evolution need not rationalize male violence against women, nor even the natural male heterosexuality that helps explain and sustain that violence. I offer other hypotheses for evolutionary theorizing in a way that reveals the value-laden character of any evolutionary claims about human beings.

In this way, *The Caveman Mystique* speaks to a debate between cultural studies scholars and scientists over the place of cultural values in scientific research and theory. Who gets to critique scientific ideas? How can we address the ways in which scientific ideas, however watered down or distorted, turn into popular culture? This book clarifies how we can—and why we must—critique the power of scientific discourse.

Evolutionary science doesn't tell a flattering story about men. More significant, many people don't understand that it's a *story*. That is why, ultimately, this book suggests that we need not only a new narrative of masculinity, but a new narrative about science. We need a new understanding of men and morality, of the relationship between science and culture, and of the relationship between bodies and discourses. As chapter 5 elaborates, my project posits that feminist scholars have something important to say about both masculinity and science. Scientists have insisted their work be critiqued or reviewed only by those with the proper *scientific* expertise. But this project insists upon the importance of cultural studies scholarship on sexuality, violence, identity, and the body for assessing scientific claims about topics increasingly popular among HBE scholars: rape, sexual harassment, and male sexual promiscuity. Amid the many scientists and nonscientists offering evolutionary explanations for men's sexual aggression, it's time for scholars of gender and culture to assert with chest-beating confidence that we can and should assess such claims. In suggesting a new way to see evolutionary science, I also offer a new vision of manhood that moves beyond the emptiness of the caveman mystique, a great leap forward I call *Homo textual*.

1

SPERM WARS, SEX WARS, AND SCIENCE WARS

Downsized Cavemen Going Apeshit

Why would men feel comforted, rather than insulted, by discussions establishing the evolutionary basis for lecherous behaviors like ogling, infidelity, and rape? I want to begin to answer that question by locating the appeal of evolutionary claims about male sexual aggression in a culture of economic downsizing and men's slipping privilege. The 1990s was a decade in which American men expressed anxiety over lost turf. Of course, men in previous decades also expressed anxiety and had crises—indeed, some scholars suggest that masculinity is never a crisis-free identity.[1] The recent wave of male anxiety is tied to economic changes and women's complaints of sexual harassment and other forms of discrimination. As women's demands gained attention, the opportunities for them expanded, but the overall economic gains for male workers telescoped. This meant that many men, especially those without college educations, began to lose their economic footing—particularly relative to women, whose earnings increased during the 1980s.

In her book *Stiffed*, Susan Faludi shows that men's frustrations stemmed from not just psychological changes, but economic ones.[2] An economic recession in the early 1980s and early 1990s, as well as the continued stagnation of real wages earned by men since the 1970s, left American male workers in a compromised position. Overall, women have seen increases in real incomes since 1973 while men have not. Broken down by educational level, men with college educations saw their incomes increase at the same rate as women's regardless of educational level. Men without a college education were doing worse economically after 1973, while women were doing better.

Both married and unmarried women's likelihood of working in the paid labor force has increased. Additionally, the wage gap between women and men closed significantly.[3] The men with full-time, year-round employment saw their incomes level off between 1981 and 1990, but during that same period, the average incomes of their female counterparts (full-time, year-round employees) increased 16.7 percent.[4] Men found themselves less likely to earn between $24,000 and $48,000 in 1989 (44.9 percent) than in 1979 (53.4 percent). In contrast, more women (34.9 percent) in 1989 had average earnings in that same "crucial middle" range of incomes than in 1979, when 26.6 percent of women's incomes fell in that range.[5]

Faludi argues that this economic downturn affecting men in particular left them feeling powerless, hopeless, and angry.[6] Many men who once had the opportunity to do meaningful work that, however dangerous, helped people or made the world run saw those opportunities slip away and be replaced by low-paying service work. These service-sector men must define themselves differently. The shift from a culture of production to a culture of consumption means that masculinity is now about appearance and scripts—an identity proffered by the capitalist marketplace—rather than the solid, contributing-member-of-society character enjoyed by men of the industrial era.[7] Service-sector men are supposed to be happy, not with responsibility or the ability to protect, provide, and sacrifice, but with appearance. Being content with your youth, attractiveness, money, posture, and swagger was an attitude American women were sold in the 1950s and eventually rejected as existentially limiting.

I remember being puzzled upon receiving a newsletter from some male college friends who had started a rock band. The newsletter for their fans portrayed the band members as having a lifestyle revolving around booze, easy women, and, of course, rock 'n' roll. But I knew these guys: they attended competitive colleges where they studied hard, did not drink often, and respected women. I knew that one had a master's degree in product packaging, and another worked as the office assistant for an executive (who admittedly hired my friend for his looks).

I later met another man, this one in a honky-tonk band, whose Web site for fans portrayed him in a similarly deceptive way. To the fans, he was a man from a broken home who hit the road driving an 18-wheeler. Yet, in reality he went to college, had happily married parents, and had for years worked smack dab in the middle of the service sector as a bookstore manager. Though such misrepresentations confused and amused me initially, I now understand them to be signals of a changing economy and changing masculinity. My friends were marketing their masculinity as they marketed their music; they knew that what sells to young male fans is not a feminized, service-sector masculinity, but an industrial-era, hands-on man pursuing whiskey, women, and work with reckless abandon. They also understood implicitly that masculinity is a fiction peddled to men in the capitalist marketplace.

Masculinity is now more about appearances and consuming than building, contributing, and producing. It's hardly that most men today find themselves raising children at home while female partners bring home the bacon, or that men today just started shopping. But, like the 1950s housewife, more men must now find satisfaction despite working below their potential (given that their job skills have lost their position to technology or other labor sources) in a postindustrial service economy that is less rewarding both materially and morally. The contemporary man now has the existential opportunities and social usefulness of the 1950s housewife. As Faludi puts it,

> The fifties housewife, stripped of her connections to a wider world and invited to fill the void with shopping and the ornamental display of her ultrafemininity, could be said to have morphed into the nineties man, stripped of his connections to a wider world and invited to fill the void with consumption and a gym-bred display of his ultra-masculinity.[8]

Men today face finding an identity in a culture of ornament.[9]

I suggest that the caveman is just such a masculine identity available to these men in crisis. The caveman is one kind of ornamental display of masculinity, a glamorous expression. The caveman mystique is that sense of one's manhood as inherently productive, protective, aggressive, and heterosexual. It represents the artifice of identities, and men's flight from artifice, as unsatisfying. As men confront economic recessions that render them socially impotent, at least by the standards that postwar American culture had promised, the caveman ethos offers them a reassuring identity as virile warriors, manly men.[10]

In "The Decline of Patriarchy," Barbara Ehrenreich explains that fewer and fewer American men rule over wives and children.[11] She identifies the drop in male wages as the main reason male-dominated households are beginning to be a thing of the past, but adds several other causes that themselves are hard to separate from the drop in men's earnings: the rise in dual-income households, the rise in the average age of first marriage, and the rise in female-headed households.[12] The fact that more women have entered the paid labor force in the past few decades has less to do with any change in women's empowerment or ambition for wage labor and more to do with economic declines among men without college educations, which has made two incomes instead of one necessary for a family to get by.[13]

Moreover, American men's interest in supporting women and children has weakened, as has the attitude that women need protection. Ehrenreich suggests that since the 1950s we've seen a male flight from women, where women are experienced as the entrapping, civilizing forces of a masculinity defined oppositionally as free and adventurous.[14] Showing that the drip-dry shirt and the TV dinner haven't received their due as the culture-changing technologies they may have been, Ehrenreich argues that the 1950s marked the time when American men no longer had to depend on women for their very survival.

The 1950s also marked the time when consumption became a legitimately masculine activity, symbolized by Hugh Hefner's playboy ethos and the movie character James Bond, who knew as much about fine wines as he did about women. A sports car or a state-of-the-art home entertainment system could now display successful manhood as well as only an attractive home maintained by a trophy wife could have done a few decades before. Like Faludi, Ehrenreich notes a shift to a consumer model of masculinity. This opened up a socially legitimate space for men to enjoy the fruits of their labor without getting married and having families—as exemplified by the playboy. In Ehrenreich's terms, the moral climate of America that had "honored, in men, responsibility, self-discipline and a protective commitment to women and children," now "endorsed[s] irresponsibility, self-indulgence and an isolationist detachment from the claims of others."[15]

Like Faludi and Ehrenreich, sociologist Neal King points to men's sense of "losing ground" in his analysis of social shifts related to masculinity and, in particular, to explain the logic of violent, male cop-action movies popular among American men in the 1990s. Cop-action movies play into concerns that only straight white men can have, namely "a bitterness toward a world that has betrayed them and called them oppressor, while moving into their occupational turf, challenging their public authority, and abandoning them at home."[16]

As that sense of losing ground makes cop-action movies and their fantasy of masculine, heroic violence pleasurable, so it also makes what Faludi calls "monstrous displays" appealing to men: "As the male role has diminished amid a sea of betrayed promises, many men have found themselves driven to more domineering and some even 'monstrous' displays in their frantic quest for a meaningful showdown."[17] The sense of losing ground can make violent fantasies (as in cop-action movies) appealing, or it can erupt in outright violence, as it did in the case of Shawn Nelson in 1995:

> A former serviceman whose career in an army tank unit had gone nowhere, a former plumber who had lost his job and whose tools had been stolen, a former husband whose wife had left him, the thirty-five-year-old Nelson broke into the National Guard armory, commandeered a fifty-seven-ton M-60 army tank, and drove it through the streets of San Diego—flattening fire hydrants, crushing forty cars, downing traffic lights and enough utility poles to cut off electricity to five thousand people. He was at war with the domestic world that he once thought he was meant to build, serve, and defend.[18]

The caveman mystique is yet another monstrous display. Like the sexual assailant in New York City mentioned in this volume's introduction, a man can enact that monstrous display on a woman whom he sees as fair game for his unstoppable animal instincts. In other cases, it can be a fantasy of who one is, or of why other men are the way they are.

Moral Disdain for Men

Another social trend is significant for the emergence of the caveman mystique. Starting with the 1970s feminist movement, but especially through the 1990s, a growing antirape movement took men to task for the problem of sexual violence against women. More state and federal dollars supported efforts to stop such violence, and men increasingly feared complaints and repercussions for those complaints. The rape trials of Mike Tyson and William Kennedy Smith Jr., the increasingly common school shootings (executed overwhelmingly by boys), the sexual harassment of women by men at the Citadel military college in South Carolina, the media attention given to the notorious Spurr Posse (a gang of guys who sought sex for "points" at almost all costs), the sexual harassment allegations against Supreme Court justice nominee Clarence Thomas, the White House sex scandals involving President Bill Clinton, and the local sexual assault trials of countless high school and college athletic stars meant more lost ground. Indeed, the 1990s saw relentless—though not necessarily ill-founded—criticism of men's sexual violence and other forms of aggression. Men's manhood seemed to take the blame for everything from school shootings to gang violence to date rape while, as Faludi points out, men's economic and social crisis has remained invisible—even to many men.[19]

Right-wing leaders and antifeminist activists were also upset with men. Those opposing abortion rights argued that sexual intercourse without procreation was undermining male responsibility, and those opposing women's equal-rights legislation argued that women's liberation would only allow men to relinquish their economic obligations to their families, sending women and children into divorce-induced poverty.[20] Considering that critics of men come from the political right and left, and from among men as well as women, it seems fair to say that in turn-of-the-millennium America, moral disdain for men—whatever their age, race, or economic rank—had reached an all-time high.

In response, some men formed their own men's groups—sometimes to bash women or feminism, sometimes just to emphasize men's strong suits, and sometimes to claim men's inner rudeness. Television networks created the rude dude: think of Howard Stern, *The Man Show,* and the obnoxious men of MTV's *Jackass,* and seemingly unending shows about college spring break. It is perhaps no wonder, then, that evolutionary narratives spoke to these intense conversations about both men's wrongdoings and strengths. Theories from the field of human behavior and evolution (HBE) appeal because they seem to many to provide reasonable, presumably objective, insights into hotly contested political issues.

HBE theorists offered their ideas in part to help society address and remedy the violence and other problems so many have been blaming on men. What HBE theorists didn't predict is that so many average Joes would take up their ideas for slightly different reasons—namely as a monstrous display, a move to feel domineering in a world squeezing men's resources and demanding that they be civil. This complex convergence of historical and political factors explains the acceptance, consumption, and popular spread of evolutionary knowledge about men.

The caveman ethos may be experienced as a concrete action or as just a fantasy. It can also be an explanatory narrative. For instance, if economic and social changes have made bachelorhood more appealing (or simply more likely) than the monogamous marriage model, what better than a Darwinian theory of innate male promiscuity to rationalize the revolt against the role of breadwinner? Before considering further the cultural appropriations of scientific HBE discourse, I want to review the basic evolutionary theory of human male sexuality.

Sperm Wars

HBE theorists argue that sexual behavior is worth examining from an evolutionary point of view. They begin by recognizing that *Homo sapiens* is a sexy species. We are relatively hairless ("naked apes," as Desmond Morris famously put it[21]), and we have no rutting season so can have sex anytime we want, even face-to-face if we'd like to. The catch is, what makes each sex sexy is different. Men are sexy for their strength and vigor, women for their beauty and coy charms. David Buss' oft-cited cross-cultural studies tell us that, the world over, men prefer beauty in their mates while women look for wealth in theirs.[22] In HBE theory, the reason for this difference comes down to our male ancestors' competition for mates, which comes down to evolution and adaptation.

Let me explain the basic idea of evolution before I get into the specifics of how it turned men into wanton skirt chasers. It would be impossible in this chapter to provide a comprehensive overview of the field or of evolutionary theories of human behavior. Entire textbooks, journals, and college courses are devoted to the subject. Instead, I will trace here the basic elements of HBE thought, particularly as it applies to human sexual behavior and, as evolutionary psychologists phrase it, the differential sexual psychologies of human males and females.[23]

Evolution by natural selection is Charles Darwin's theory that variations that inhibit an individual's ability to survive to maturity and reproduce will be eliminated.[24] For example, giraffes with slightly longer necks will survive a "hostile environment" of tall trees, reproduce more giraffes with slightly longer necks, and so on, gradually eliminating variation in giraffe neck length. As HBE scholars Martin Daly and Margo Wilson note in *Sex, Evolution, and Behavior,* "All species *overproduce* offspring, not all of which can survive to reproduce in their turn. Thus, there is inevitable competition among the individuals of each species for the means to survive and reproduce, and any inherited advantage in this competition will be naturally selected."[25] Natural selection works on phenotypes (developmental potentials of genes, appearing as actual traits of organisms in a given environment), but the evolutionary change is transmitted by surviving genes, which are situated on chromosomes. Natural selection favors the genes, encased in people, that increase their own numbers in succeeding generations.

An adaptation is that which is brought about by differentials among alternative forms, the relative advantage of the feature vis-à-vis its alternative forms playing a significant causal role in its production.[26] Some things people do are evolved traits that were put into humans' nature. Some traits were, at one point, in the environment of evolutionary adaptedness (the hunting and gathering part of our human history, which ended roughly 10,000 years ago with the spread of agriculture; hereafter EEA), passed on from one generation to the next more often than some other traits.[27] If a specific trait is adaptive, it means that those with that trait who survived to reproductive age and had children who themselves survived to reproductive age had greater reproductive success in the EEA than those who did not possess such a trait. In other words, some physical traits and psychological mechanisms, whether or not they contribute to reproductive success now, can be considered adaptations. "Human nature," then, is that hodgepodge of adaptations geared toward an Ice Age hunter–gatherer environment.[28] Behaviors and traits that were adaptive maximized inclusive fitness in the EEA. Adaptations have nothing to do with morality and, as HBE theorists acknowledge, may be seen as thoroughly corrupt from various political or religious standpoints.

Sexual reproduction enables gene recombination, and thus, provides greater genetic variety for adaptiveness in a hostile environment. For evolutionary theorists, the fact that humans are a sexually reproducing species implies the evolution of two distinct (male and female) human natures or sexual psychologies. The fact that men have many small sperm while women have relatively few large ova means that women's parental investment is much greater than men's: only women can gestate, bear, and nurse the young. In the absence of technology allowing otherwise (i.e., in the EEA), reproduction is "cheap" for men and "costly" for women. The body design that forced our foremothers to invest ovulation, gestation, and lactation time caused their greater coyness. Our forefathers, on the other hand, were not forced by their bodily design to invest much of anything and, thus, could copulate as often as they desired with little physical cost. Evolutionary theorists reason that men's great number of sperm makes them perpetually sexually interested and carefree. Choosy females, were therefore, a limiting resource for which men competed against one another.[29]

HBE theorists apply adaptationist thinking to contemporary human behavior by asking, among other things: What adaptive problems would have had to be solved for men in the ancestral environment? Why do men cheat? Why do they get jealous when their wives cheat? Was there something about the ancestral environment that made this behavior adaptive? Clearly, applying evolutionary theory to human behavior is far more speculative than, say, finding information about successful adaptations demonstrated in the fossil record or uncovering relationships between species in DNA comparisons. Nevertheless, HBE scholars see support for their hypotheses about sex-linked traits in patriarchal cultural patterns and sexist laws, such as those, in some countries, that give husbands round-the-clock sexual access to their wives or that allow men to sell women as commodities.

Where feminists say that the personal is political, evolutionary theorists would say the personal is evolutionary. Where many feminist scholars would argue that biology is cultural, evolutionary theorists would insist that culture is biology.[30] Where feminists see patterns of economic inequality and ideologies of gender in people's intimate, daily lives, evolutionary scholars find patterns of evolved desire. Where feminists would say men have power over women in sex, evolutionary theorists would say women have power over men. It is interesting to note that both HBE and feminist scholars agree that Western history is one of men aggressively seeking to control women, treating women as property, and defining women in ways that rationalize men's sexual oppression of them. This gloomy view of men characterizes many feminist, antifeminist, HBE, and right-wing claims. What distinguishes HBE theory from other accounts of sexual politics is its view that men's sexually aggressive and promiscuous behavior is rooted in human evolution.

David Barash explains this possibly uncomfortable thought in *The Whisperings Within*:

Plants that commit rape and bacteria that spoil food are following evolutionary strategies that maximize their fitness. And, clearly, in neither
case do the actors know what they are doing, or why. We human beings
like to think we are different. We introspect, we are confident that we
know what we are doing, and why. But we may have to open our minds
and admit the possibility that our need to maximize our fitness may be
whispering somewhere deep within us and that, know it or not, most of
the time we are heeding these whisperings.[31]

In the context of HBE theory, human sexuality is a complex, evolved
psychology adapted to the environment in which our ancestors lived for
most of human history. What turns us on is not simply cultural, but a call
from genes whispering from deep within. Just as the big pink estrus swell-
ing of a female baboon is attractive to male baboons, a beautiful young
woman triggers men's evolved psychological mechanisms of sexual desire.
Ancestral men who went for such women, HBE theorists reason, would
have ended up more reproductively successful than men who didn't have
the same psychology. This psychology need not make us reproductively
successful today to prove the evolutionary theorist's point. Even if a man
today chooses to wear a condom when he's lucky enough to bed a buxom
babe, in the ancestral environment (sans condoms) his actions would
clearly have maximized fitness.

So, today, regardless of reproductive success, men live out evolved
patterns of desire. This explains why men tend to place greater emphasis than do women on the physical beauty of their mates. Ancestral men
who dismissed beauty as only skin deep died out because of the compara-
tive advantage gained by men who couldn't resist the physical signals of
fertility. Ancestral women, on the other hand, would have sought males
with resources so that their children would thrive (hence, "diamonds are a
girl's best friend"). For the same reasons, men are more interested in visual
pornographic materials than women, who themselves are more interested
in the fantasies of romance novels, which emphasize relationship bonds.
Indeed, HBE theorists Catherine Salmon and Donald Symons argue that
these sex differences in erotic desires reveal the contrasting selection pressures faced by ancestral men and women.[32]

This beauty-versus-resources sex difference can also explain differing
patterns of jealousy. Michael Wiederman and Erica Kendall have published a study in the journal *Evolution and Human Behavior* showing that

women tend to get more jealous when their male partner commits *emotional infidelity* (such as falling in love with someone else), whereas men are more likely to get jealous when their female partner commits *sexual infidelity* (such as having intercourse with another man, even if it is a one-night stand).[33]

Male reproductive competition meant that ancestral men who felt possessive better ensured paternity and rights to continued access to "their" women.[34] Overall, as Wilson and Daly put it, "men take a proprietary view of women's sexuality and reproductive capacity." They contend that this pattern is an evolved "sexual psychology," a male mindset.[35] It is thus that HBE theorists chart a path from genes to brain to boner.

Even men's forcing sex on women can be explained by the sexual rivalry between men, and by women being a limiting resource in the evolutionary sense. Perhaps the most talked-about HBE book addressing male sexual aggression (human and nonhuman) is Randy Thornhill and Craig Palmer's *A Natural History of Rape*, in which the authors explain why evolutionary thinking helps us understand the prevalence of men's sexual aggression against women. For instance, men who rape tend to be in their teens and twenties, and the victims of the crime tend to be women at the ages of peak fertility. Thornhill and Palmer insist that many non-human animals rape: "Across species, the 'common denominator' in this pattern is an evolutionary history that involves greater competition among males than among females for sexual access to multiple mates, not human-like sexual socialization."[36]

Thus, they claim that social scientists who say that rape is strictly about socialization ignore the insects, birds, fish, reptiles, marine mammals, and nonhuman primates that rape.[37] The authors point out that feminist Susan Brownmiller grounded her claim—in the best-selling book *Against Our Will*—that rape is not natural in the assumption that no animals rape in their natural habitats.[38] They counter that "there is no longer any question that physical force, harassment, and intimidation are used widely by males across species, including the great apes, to obtain mates."[39]

These HBE scholars insist that social scientists who've tried to explain rape as based on male social power over women are driven by ideological concerns that are not scientific and, in particular, not properly evolutionary. Do Thornhill and Palmer want men to start forming rapist clubs and HBE scholars to start serving as expert witnesses for men on trial for rape? No. But do they insist that feminists and others they might loosely lump into a "liberal" camp deny the uncomfortable fact of men's evolved tendencies? Yes.

Apart from the cause of the problem, HBE theorists' claims about male sexual aggression seem to mesh perfectly with feminists' own criticisms of men. But, just as HBE theory took hold in academia, a huge debate in feminism had emerged over just how different men and women really were. This debate in feminism came to be known as the sex wars.

Sex Wars

Just when feminists seemed to argue too strongly that men were beastly rapists and women their hapless victims, other feminists came out of the rallies to declare this view oversimplified. Feminists argued over the legitimacy of pornography, sadomasochistic sex, and bisexuality; they debated the content of safe-sex education programs and the scope of reproductive freedom for women. Known as the "sex wars," these debates among feminists about women's sexuality reminded us of women's diverse sexual styles and desires.[40] In emphasizing their own politically incorrect desires, many of these feminists challenged not only the monolithic view of female sexuality as innocent and passive, but also, by extension, the view of male sexuality as aggressive and depraved.

HBE theorists, on the other hand, are willing to say that men are dogs. So, while many people tend to believe that feminists are man haters who think all men are potential rapists, such a view is remarkably more common among evolutionary theorists who study men. HBE theorists tend to agree with the most putatively "antimale" of the feminists, such as Catherine MacKinnon or Andrea Dworkin.[41] Both evolutionary theorists and these radical feminists agree that women are defined in terms of their sexual availability to men. The sex wars have shown, however, that not all feminists agree that this is an appropriate characterization. After all, such a view ignores the ways in which women assert sexual agency and can be aggressive, even abusive. So, not all feminists would agree with evolutionary theorists' depictions.[42]

Feminists tend to give men more credit than evolutionary theorists do, while also insisting that women are not passive dimwits who were busy baking brownies as the evolutionary record passed by. The sex wars also raised our awareness that women could be bad mothers, sexually aggressive, and violent. In this sense, the newer feminist view of women bears directly on our assessment of evolutionary theories of rape. Naomi

Weisstein has used Sarah Blaffer Hrdy's feminist evolutionary account of mothering to dispute HBE theorists Thornhill and Palmer's naive assumption that human males who raped in the EEA would have put rapist genes into the population. Weisstein notes that

> evidence from hunter–gatherer societies suggests that deep into our prehistory women knew who the fathers of their children were, and aborted, neglected, abandoned or killed those infants they did not want to raise. Children conceived by rape may have been highly valued in some cultures. Most likely, they were snuffed out before they could reach the gene pool.[43]

Another outcome of these sex wars in feminism was to question any simplistic division between men and women, a division that was fueled in part by the subset of lesbian feminists who saw men as aggressive, competitive, and otherwise to be avoided. The sex wars made room for new forms of female sexuality—including those that sought relations with men as well as practices that were masochistic or otherwise "feminine"—which meant moving beyond the construction of men as always already pigs. Sexual behavior and sex categories were understood by feminists as political issues, influenced by cultural forms and structures of domination. The sex wars involved debates over which sex acts and desires counted as normal and which as deviant, which acts were politically correct, which politically incorrect ones were actually radical political acts, and so forth. The sex wars included challenges, particularly from women who slept with men as well as women, to the categories *homosexual* and *heterosexual*. The homo/hetero divide was challenged as too simplistic for ignoring the many preferences other than the sex of one's object choice that make up sexual identity.

The sex wars of the 1980s challenged the ideas that men and women had distinct sexualities and that sexual identities were as simple as anyone on either side of the political spectrum had imagined. Any consistencies found in male and female sexuality were social constructions—that is, a result of political, economic, and cultural patterns. The relevance of this debate to my study, then, is that the sex wars already debated whether or not men were pigs, and women their virtuous, monogamous counterparts. For HBE theorists, however, a version of the sex wars is still being waged. They insist that men, in fact, are pigs, and that it has to do with evolution. Those who don't agree with them are characterized as having buried their

heads in the sands of social constructionism in an orgy of political correct-
ness bent on denying our animal origins.

In a unique volume attempting to merge feminism and evolutionary
psychology, David Buss and Neil Malamuth posit that evolutionary psychology is impartial, while feminist studies are ideological: "Evolutionary
psychology is a *scientific discipline* and hence is primarily concerned with
describing and explaining *what exists.* Feminism shares with evolutionary psychology a concern with describing and explaining what exists, but
it also carries a social and political agenda. Hence, feminism is partly
concerned with what *ought* to exist."[44] But, might evolutionary scholars
have ideological biases? And might feminist scholars have some academic
authority on matters of sexuality and gender? It is to this debate over science, politics, and academic authority that I now turn.

Science Wars

Where does a feminist sociologist get off thinking she can write a book
critiquing a scientific field? Some scientists claim that a portion of the Academic Left, including scholars like me who study science, lack an intellectually rigorous basis for critiquing them or are too political or idealistic to
do so. At the same time, many feminist critics of science have attempted
to belittle evolutionary scientists in hopes their readers will look down on
these scholars as hopeless political reactionaries. Feminists have portrayed
HBE scholars as doing "bad science," for example, painting them as sexist
men with a fascistic agenda. How did this battle between scientists and
those who study scientific claims emerge? In answering that question, I
will show that the debates over men's sexual nature are, to a significant
extent, debates over the authority of science.

The science wars gained public notice in 1996 when physicist Alan
Sokal orchestrated what came to be known as the Sokal Hoax. Paul R.
Gross and Norman Levitt's *Higher Superstition: The Academic Left and Its
Quarrels with Science* had already been published,[45] and a special issue of
the premiere cultural studies journal *Social Text* was being put together
to address the science wars. Sokal submitted a bogus deconstruction of
physics and got it published as an article in that special issue of *Social
Text*,[46] after which he exposed the article as a hoax in the (now defunct)
academic magazine *Lingua Franca*.[47] That his intentionally ridiculous
critique of physics made it into *Social Text* without being reviewed by a

physicist meant, to Sokal, that science studies lacked bona fide scholarly standards.[48]

Science studies was already an established multidisciplinary academic field, and scientists like Sokal were angry.[49] Sokal, like some of his colleagues, resented the criticisms of science made by those in science studies. Their beef was that one should be a scientist, not a literary critic or a sociologist, in order to comment on scientific claims. Gross and Levitt, a biologist and mathematician, respectively, have argued that feminist, Marxist, multiculturalist, social constructionist, and radical environmentalist scholars comprise an "academic left" that has produced "turgid and opaque" claims and "tooth-fairy hypotheses," which amount to so much "hermeneutic hootchy-koo." In contrast, they claim that scientists are not ideological, but rather seek to produce "objective truth about the world" and "rigorous" and "reliable factual knowledge."[50]

Scholars from a variety of disciplines—sociology, history, political science, philosophy, women's studies, ethnic studies, literature, and cultural studies—have produced a vast collection of books and articles that examine the ways in which science has participated in troubling practices and created differences that rationalize domination, in addition to chronicling paradigm shifts or the life and times of particular scientists. Scientists like Sokal don't object to feminists and others pointing out when a scholar does "bad science" because he had sexist assumptions—when, for instance, a scientist's own sexist bias kept him from adhering to the rules of scientific inquiry.[51] Neither would they mind, presumably, those science studies investigations of the impact of science, medicine, and technology on gender relations. (For instance, a study of Viagra from a feminist perspective doesn't dispute the science of the drug itself or how scientists designed the drug, but rather examines the social implications of men taking the drug to get an erection, the effect of that drug on how sex and sexual intimacy get defined, the marketing of that drug, and so on.[52]) It's the studies of science that actually criticize the contents of the scientific inquiry, and that assume that science is inescapably political, that rile many scientists. Sokal and his supporters would have people believe that such leftists and feminists who study science engage in their own intellectually weak and politically driven project—a reverse social Darwinism, if you will, by which, no matter what the evidence, they will insist that men and women are, deep down, the same.

In the revelation of his hoax on *Social Text*, Sokal challenges social constructionists by saying that "anyone who believes that the laws of physics are social conventions is invited to try transgressing those conventions from the windows of my apartment."[53] But, of course, social constructionists never said that, if you jump out a window, you won't fall to the ground.[54] As science studies scholar Steve Fuller puts it, when we say that gravity is a concept and that there are other ways of explaining the same phenomenon, some scientists hear, "Gravity exists only in our minds and, if we thought otherwise, we could fall up not down."[55]

Of course, many feminist scholars exhibit that same type of knee-jerk reaction to anything an HBE theorist says. For example, when an HBE theorist says that a specific behavior is an adaptation, some feminists hear, "That behavior is unchangeable and morally right because it came from nature." And when an HBE theorist says that there may have been no selective pressure against male sexual aggression, some feminists hear, "Nature intended for men to rape and so feminists should stop struggling against such misdeeds and women should lie back and enjoy them." Feminists and other critics of HBE ideas are also likely to claim that evolutionary psychologists and other HBE theorists are "not really scientists." For example, the collected essays in Cheryl Travis's *Evolution, Gender, and Rape*, criticizing Thornhill and Palmer's *A Natural History of Rape*, frame the HBE theory behind it as bad science.[56]

Such a framing never challenges the cognitive authority enjoyed by science; it only attempts to move the rhetorical line demarcating "good" or "real" scientists, who presumably deserve intellectual authority and whose interpretations of nature should be trusted. Thomas Gieryn notes that "so secure is the epistemic authority of science these days, that even those who would dispute another's scientific understanding of nature must ordinarily rely on science to muster a persuasive challenge."[57] The main question asked during the Sokal hoax was whether or not non-scientists should have a scientist review their work in order to be more careful in their claim making. But the science wars also raise the related question: Should scientists have as much authority as they do to comment on cultural issues? After all, how often does anyone ever take HBE theorists to task for not having a women's studies scholar, sociologist, or queer theorist review manuscripts about the evolutionary basis for men's ogling of women?

Scientists can be seen as neutral scholars asking about neutral, biological issues only if we see the body as disconnected from history and culture. However, understanding complex cultural arrangements, such as gender, sexuality, and violence, requires another kind of expertise. The analysis of rape serves to illustrate the expertise feminist scholars can contribute to attempts to understand the problem from within the theory of evolution.

Feminist scholarship has long shown that the overwhelming majority of rapes are committed by acquaintances, friends, family members, and lovers of the victims and, significantly, often without weapons or even the awareness that they are doing anything violent. HBE scholars shoot feminists down by saying that they mistakenly think rape is an act of violence, not an act of sex. This idea that rape is an act of violence was meant to convey—in a move that may be too far outside the box for our male-centered culture—the victim's, rather than the perpetrator's, experience of the event. (Who said the two have the same experience of the event?) I do not naively think that men aren't sexually aroused in rape—a point HBE scholars often make, as if showing that rape feels sexual to men indicates that it may be an adaptation.

Indeed, I rely on the research of Diana Scully, a feminist social scientist, that shows the alarming proportion of convicted rapists who, from their jail cell, told Scully they had had sex with the woman/accuser, but that it had been consensual—even those who'd stuck a knife to their victims' throats.[58] Obviously, if many of these men imagined their acts of forced sex as consensual and sexy, we can assume that this view characterizes huge numbers of young men who have raped without weapons, such as those who have raped their dates. That a man may experience rape as sexually arousing does not make it "natural" or driven. That a man experiences rape as sexy does not negate that it is, for his victim, an act of violence.

In characterizing social scientists as denying that rape is *sexually* motivated, Thornhill and Palmer misunderstand the heart of the feminist analysis of rape, which is that rape is as sexual as consensual sex is power laden.[59] Put differently, in our rape culture, which celebrates male domination as erotic, a man's having power over a woman is what feeling sexy is all about. Thornhill and Palmer quote Peggy Reeves Sanday, a feminist scholar concerned with the culture surrounding rape in the United States, who says that during a rape "the sexual act is not concerned with sexual gratification, but with the deployment of the penis as a concrete symbol of masculine social power."[60] Some feminists have also pointed out that during consensual sex the penis is deployed in the same manner.[61] In fact Thornhill and Palmer quote Tim Beneke, who argues that "sex itself often has little to do with sex."[62] Beneke's point is that sex, like rape, has cultural meanings attached to it. But Thornhill and Palmer set up a false dichotomy between meanings and bodies, between culture and nature—as though, if they can show that men find rape physically arousing, then it must have a biological cause.

Assuming that the corporeal aspects of sexuality must be its biological, evolved dimension, Thornhill and Palmer misunderstand the more general idea that sexuality is wrapped up with a search for self-identity.[63] They think feminists are saying that men aren't physically aroused if they're trying to be men, or if they're thinking of themselves as dominant. Profeminist writer and activist John Stoltenberg has argued convincingly to the contrary: that men in our culture tend to have sex in order to have *a sex*, which is to say that men use sexual intercourse with women to experience themselves as being male.[64] He posits that this eroticized social dominance is precisely what men must reconsider in order to transform our rape culture, and urges men to think of their role in sexual relations with women as *being the friend there* rather than as *being the man there*.

Thornhill and Palmer miss the point of Beneke, Stoltenberg, and other feminist scholars who show that these meanings are tied to bodily reactions. We can't separate our bodily reactions from cultural meanings. Claiming that a man experiences meaning in connection to his sexual act is no more or less evolutionary than claiming that a mother experiences meaning in raising her child. Thornhill and Palmer so drastically misconstrue the feminist position that they appear at least as guilty of the ideological motivations of which they accuse feminists. However, in Thornhill and Palmer's case, the ideological investment is not in sexism or male social control, as many feminists would suggest. The ideological investment lies in *the authority of science*.

What role do authoritative scientific claims play in the meanings men attach to sexual violence? Even if our male ancestors raped women, they certainly did not do so with the rationale of evolutionary science in their own heads. Indeed, this level of self-reflection—the establishment of an embodied masculine identity negotiated through various forms of expert knowledge all claiming who and why men are the way they are—sets humans apart, not only from our nonhuman kin, but also from humans in other historical eras.

In suggesting that I have authority to speak about rape, I am not suggesting that I also be granted the right to talk about genetics without any training in that field. I am suggesting that scientists' claims about gender, sexuality, violence, and culture—about which they have had little, if any, scholarly training—be modified by scholars who have legitimate authority on these matters. I insist that feminist scholars have something important to say about human bodies, and by extension the scientific claims that explain our bodies. Thus, my critique of science is less my encroachment into "their" territory than it is a critique of their encroachment into mine.

A common belief is that politics and science should ideally be separate. Science studies scholars argue that science, with its history of skull-size measurements comparing blacks unfavorably to whites, its measurements of the putatively extralarge genitalia of lesbians, and its textbook descriptions of aggressive sperm competing to swim to a passive egg in waiting is from the start already a tad political. Science has drawn moral boundaries; social movements for the rights of women, gay men and lesbians, and people of color make this more obvious because their visions have often clashed.

New social movements have been challenging common assumptions about gender and sexuality, insisting that scholars of all types look at identities differently. In addition to concerns with emancipation from enslaving social systems, new social movements have challenged ways of thinking and acting.[65] As such they have challenged the authority of science to define who we are. For example, the women's movement challenged scientific and medical authorities that assumed women to be passive compared to men, or that positioned women as nurturing and more naturally capable parents. Gays and lesbians challenged scientific constructions of homosexuality as abnormal. Some, embracing the "queer" label, have challenged the scientific division of people into the categories *homosexual* and *heterosexual*. These social movements have challenged the hegemonic authority of science, and some scientists are angry.

Some HBE scholars attempt to stay out of the fray by saying it's not up to them to discuss the social consequences of their academic theories. I insist that these academics have a responsibility to realize that they work in a political context and that their ideas have consequences. Their oft-repeated saying that "*is* doesn't lead to *ought*" is a cop-out. Besides, like it or not, science has values and background assumptions. The ideas that people have gender and sexual identities, that sexuality revolves around gender identities, and that the sex of one's object choice organizes a person's sexual preference are cultural claims, not natural facts.

The debates over science's role in social change or oppression and the place of values in science have a long history. In fact, as I show in chapter 2, Darwin's theory sparked a debate on this very topic. Just as the current political, economic, and social milieu affects how evolutionary narratives about who we are get taken up, a very different social milieu in the mid-nineteenth century produced a very different reception of Darwin's theory of evolution by natural selection. It is to this social reception of Darwin's theory that I now turn, showing that over a century's time evolution came to be seen as a moral answer, a new religion with which to tell the truth of who we are.

2

HOMO RESURRECTUS

THE THEORY OF EVOLUTION AS A MORAL ANSWER FOR MEN

Darwin's Theory and the Crisis in Morals

Human life, in the evolutionary sense, is a mistake.[1] It is accidental, unplanned, a product of a variety of chance processes—a fluke. For decades after his *On the Origin of Species* appeared in 1859, Charles Darwin's theory of evolution by natural selection threatened many people who believed that living things were guided by the divine. The idea that evolution had no moral logic—that any old trait could have emerged through selective pressure—undermined the inclination to ground moral or political claims in some absolute framework, specifically the dominant religious one. I'll discuss some of this worried debate from Darwin's day in this chapter. I'll also show that, over a century's time, evolution came to be seen as a new religion, a moral answer to the very crisis that evolutionary thinking instigated, and by extension a moral answer about men's bad behaviors.

Debates over science and morality did not begin in 1859 with Darwin's *Origin of Species,* nor did theories of evolution. But Darwin's theory of evolution was unique in that it provided an explanation of how species became modified—that is, through natural selection. This is a mechanistic process and, thus, excluded from nature any creative force.[2] Darwin's view portrayed a nature shaped entirely by blind chance. As historian of science Stephen Jay Gould has put it, "The details of the natural world lay in a realm of contingency undirected by laws that set the channels."[3] Evolution by natural selection implies that the world is run by a trial and error process (natural selection) rather than a divine engineer (God).[4] Darwin's theory brought to a head a crisis in moral thought that had been developing for two centuries.

Christianity had been under attack by science since Galileo countered the Catholic Church's view that the sun revolved around the earth. Indeed, educated people in Darwin's day had already read arguments that the Bible was myth and that God was man's creation, rather than vice versa.[5] Modern science increasingly came to be seen as the road to truth, and Darwinism came to be seen as a great threat to religion. Darwin himself had few enemies, and his supporters often tried to explain how Darwin's views meshed with those of Christianity.[6] At the same time, however, some popularizers of Darwin's work were more hostile to religion, and many Christians believed their views irreconcilable with Darwin's.[7]

Many thought the theory of evolution by natural selection took the meaning and purpose—thus, the enchantment—from their lives. How would people maintain a belief in right and wrong if humans were not created and inspired by God? As James Bixby wrote in his 1891 book *The Crisis in Morals*, "The time-honored principles of ethics that recognized the moral sense as innate, the verdicts of conscience as authoritative, and the sanctions of morality as God-given, are daily discredited."[8] Many learned men in the United States and Europe felt demoralized in the wake of Darwin's theory of evolution by natural selection. Countless books and letters were written by these disenchanted men. Their anxieties were twofold: first, if humans lacked a soul and a place above nature, then they were insignificant and morally disrespectable; second, if they lacked a divine basis for telling right from wrong, then they faced an unnerving inability to make moral distinctions.

Both of these anxieties relate to a further problem with Darwinian implications about sex and interpersonal relationships. Darwin's work seemed to imply that heterosexual reproduction was a haphazard meeting of sperm and egg; the union of man and woman was not divinely inspired or holy, but instead lusty, animalistic, and random. People did not morally approve of what they saw other species doing, sexually and otherwise. This led botanist and theologian Asa Gray, in 1860, to write Darwin on the atheistic implications of his theory:

"I am bewildered. . . . There seems to me too much misery in the world. I cannot persuade myself that a beneficent and omnipotent God would have designedly created the Ichneumonidae with the express intention of their feeding within the living bodies of Caterpillars, or that a cat should play with mice. . . ."[9]

Darwin himself wrote to Joseph Dalton Hooker in 1856, "What a book a devil's chaplain might write on the clumsy, wasteful, blundering, low and horribly cruel works of nature."[10] In 1889, biology professor Thomas H. Huxley lamented over man really being made in the image of a gorilla:

I know of no story which is so utterly saddening as that of the evolution of humanity. Man emerges with the marks of his lowly origin strong upon him. He is a brute, only more intelligent than other brutes, a blind prey to impulses, which as often as not lead him to destruction; a victim to endless illusion, which make his mental existence a terror and a burden, and fill his physical life with barren toil and battle.[11]

Gray reconciled his troubles the way Darwin was said to have done by the end of his life, and the way the majority of Americans do today: by concluding that a deity rather than chance is responsible for the course of evolution.[12] People then and now have been compelled to believe that God steered evolution because they assume that a divine volitional side to nature is necessary for moral purpose.[13] Indeed, conceiving nature without God threatened to introduce moral chaos. Geology professor Adam Sedgwick wrote to Darwin, who had been his student, about his apparent aim of divorcing God from nature, the moral from the material, saying that humanity "would suffer a damage that might brutalize it, and sink the human race into a lower grade of degradation than any into which it has fallen since its written records tell us of its history."[14]

Men seemed to feel this panic more acutely than women, but then, in the nineteenth century, men enjoyed more opportunities than women to publish their thoughts. Still, though, the breakdown of what seemed like a unified worldview and a moral consensus arguably threatened mainly those with the privilege to imagine that such a consensus had actually existed—namely, white Western men. Those oppressed by Christian discourse and hit in the face with Western values—Africans who were colonized or enslaved, for instance, or privileged men's wives and daughters, who had relatively few legal rights—might have welcomed the collapse of the old moral regime, or at least would not have had as strong a reason to believe that a moral consensus characterized their world.

Although many accepted Darwin's theory, some of the most privileged men felt threatened by the idea that their origins were natural. Learned men's disdain for an identity as animals had to do with their privileged position in society and the world. After all, white Western men had been rationalizing systems of slavery and colonial rule on the grounds that the black people they oppressed were animals or, at best, a subspecies of humans. Of course, the white people who resisted Darwin's theory also faced the paradox of insisting that all men were God's creation, thereby linking them more closely to the so-called savage races. For this reason some insisted that the human races were distinct species so as to set humans apart from animals while also allowing white people to retain their view of themselves as superior to people of color.[15] There is much scholarly documentation of the frightening ways in which huge numbers of white people managed to reduce the ethics of slavery down to the equivalent of eating a hamburger. For our purposes here, the salient point is that white men had a lot riding on *not* being like black people— and for some this meant denying Darwin's theory altogether.

People also resisted seeing their sexuality in Darwinian terms. After all, from the point of view of Victorian sexual ideology, apes and monkeys were obscene. Indeed, the Enlightenment served to challenge the reigning biblical view of sex. Darwin's theory, specifically, shifted what had been a religious order of mating into a natural order of mating.

In *The Descent of Man, and Selection in Relation to Sex* (1871), Darwin discussed the idea of sexual selection, applying it to humans in the very last chapters of his book. There he described the interest in ornament of so-called primitive tribes, the racial traits of various groups, and the human male's superiority over females in strength and intelligence. (Notably, but not surprising given the times, Darwin thought what women lacked in intellectual capacity men lacked in moral qualities.[16]) Darwin asked how we might account for the distinctive features of the two sexes and the distinctive features of racial groups. He also went over many studies describing sexual selection in insects, fish, reptiles, birds, and mammals. Sexual selection concerns both the competition among members of the same sex for breeding access to the other sex and the mating preferences revealed by a sex. The peacock's conspicuous plumage does not give the bird a survival advantage (indeed, such colorful feathers attract predators), but a specifically reproductive advantage. Men and women are different from one another because of sexual selection—a natural process of reproductive success—and not God's design.

With the idea of divinely inspired heterosexual bonds under threat, people now wondered what would curb licentious sexual behaviors. Given the panicky debate over the ethical implications of Darwin's dangerous ideas, thinkers of the day eagerly sought to create a new moral system, or at least urged other intellectuals to do so. Herbert Spencer, another notable evolutionist, commented,

> Now that moral injunctions are losing the authority given by their supposed sacred origin, the secularization of morals is becoming imperative. Few things can happen more disastrous than the decay and death of a regulative system no longer fit, before another and fitter regulative system has grown up to replace it.[17]

It did not take long for various philosophers, scientists, and religious leaders to look to science, and evolution specifically, for answers; C. M. Williams wrote, "By far the most important and most difficult demand which practical philosophy makes upon the theory of evolution seems to be that of a new theory of morals."[18]

Darwinism as the Second Coming

Certainly Darwin did not cause the death of Christianity, but increasingly people turned from the Bible to some form of evolution for moral guidance.[19] Anatomist and anthropologist Sir Arthur Keith declared, "The Darwinists' Bible is the great book of Nature. Creeds will come and go, but this is the book that will endure as long as life lasts."[20] If Darwin's theory prompted a crisis in morals, including sexual regulation, scientific endeavor would restore an earlier theocentric unity and thereby put an end to this crisis with a new foundation for ethics. Darwinism could become the new religion. And so, divinely inspired ethics eventually gave way to naturalistic ethics.[21] Nature, rather than God, became the source of morality.

Turning science into the solution to the crisis in morals never challenged the existential anxieties over a lack of ultimate purpose and truth. Science simply became the new source of moral meaning. Keith, for instance, made evolution into his religion while finding a way to resolve the issue of "evil:"

We human beings are the subjects of her [nature's] experiment—the pawns of her great game. She sacrifices her pawns without compunction in order to win her game. It is here that the religion of the Darwinist comes to his aid: it helps him to understand the apparent injustices of the game of life. Not that his religion is one of pure resignation. He watches Nature at play to learn if it be possible to modify the rules of her game. He learns and hopes to accomplish his object. This, too, is part of the faith and religion of a Darwinist.[22]

One way to turn Darwinism into a secular extension of Christian thought was to view evolution in a hierarchical manner, with humans at the apex of a progressive ladder, seeing some ultimate moral purpose that was difficult to extract from the view of evolution as meaningless change. Darwin's sentiments accomplish this:

Man may be excused for feeling some pride at having risen, though not through his own exertions, to the very summit of the organic scale; and the fact of having thus risen, instead of having been aboriginally placed there, may give him hope for a still higher destiny in the distant future.[23]

Bixby's conceptualizations also achieve this:

The peculiarity of life is its pressure toward larger and higher existence. The measure and purpose of progress is the unfolding of higher consciousness.... The test of what is morally good is the tendency of the given motive to help forward the progress of the race toward the ideal perfection of humanity. Those motives are bad which would impede this progress.... The vital solidarity of the individual with the Universal Life supplies to ethics an objective foundation and an authority as real as it is felt to be supreme.[24]

The social, ethical, and political implications of Darwinism made it incredibly popular by the late 1800s. In his study of German popular Darwinism between 1860 and 1914, historian Alfred Kelly concludes that "every Darwinist became ipso facto a social theorist."[25] Marxists, for example, interpreted Darwinism to mean that economic inequalities thwarted people's abilities to reach their true potential. Some conservatives, on the other hand, thought Darwinism meant that economic struggle and inequality were natural and, hence, just.[26]

Darwin's theory was applied to programs of population control. This included the nineteenth-century German science of "racial hygiene," which informed the abominable practice of genocide in Nazi Germany. In the early twentieth century a U.S. eugenics movement encouraged policies and practices enabling the "fit" people to breed and discouraging, if not oppressively preventing, those seen as intellectually and physically inferior from reproducing—all in the name of creating a better, healthier society.

At the time such advocacy was not necessarily seen as conservative or right-wing; such policies were advocated by people who considered themselves progressives, including the famous birth control advocate Margaret Sanger. Sanger's victories for legalizing some forms of birth control can be credited more to eugenics than to feminism. The eugenics movement appealed to many privileged white people as sensible public health policy during a time when non-WASP immigrant populations swelled. Eugenics was a subject studied in American universities and was popular in other ways. For instance, county fairs held "Fitter Family" contests, sponsored by the American Eugenics Society, in which people were rewarded for appearing "fit" in the Darwinian sense.[27] Books encouraged men to select the "right"—that is, the "fittest"— women as partners for the healthiest children. The book *Heredity and You* even provided a drawing of the type of woman men should seek (see fig. 2.1). The eugenically fit woman was not the ideal beauty, but a robust breeder.

Eugenics died out in the United States with the rise of Adolf Hitler's atrocities. Even Darwinian theory went into hibernation due to postwar distaste for biological theories of hierarchy.[28] But decades later, several developments in the scholarly study of evolution gave rise to new scholarship on evolution applied to humans, which made Darwinism more interesting and, once again, morally vexing.

In 1966, George Williams published *Adaptation and Natural Selection,* which argues that group selection did not play the role in evolution that had been previously assumed; adaptations are *individual* rather than group ones, including, even, altruism: if being a good friend maximizes an *individual's* evolutionary advantage, then animals and humans are not as purely altruistic as earlier scholars asserted.[29] Selection might favor people who can be good friends, but only because such a trait ultimately confers a selfish advantage.

Two key moments shaping contemporary human behavior and evolution (HBE) theory followed Williams' book: the publication of William Hamilton's work on kinship and Robert Trivers' work on reciprocity.[30] In 1964, Hamilton wrote about the implication of the advances in population genetics for social behavior and morality. He explained the role of

DESIRABLE TRAITS IN WOMEN

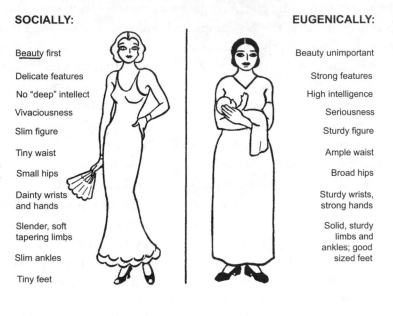

SOCIALLY: EUGENICALLY:

Beauty first   Beauty unimportant

Delicate features   Strong features

No "deep" intellect   High intelligence

Vivaciousness   Seriousness

Slim figure   Sturdy figure

Tiny waist   Ample waist

Small hips   Broad hips

Dainty wrists   Sturdy wrists,
and hands   strong hands

Slender, soft   Solid, sturdy
tapering limbs   limbs and
                                                 ankles; good
Slim ankles   sized feet

Tiny feet

Fig. 2.1   Desirable Traits.

kinship in the evolution of social behavior and termed any ability to get one's own genes represented in future generations "inclusive fitness." In 1971, Trivers provided a theoretical framework for interpreting animals' social behavior with his work on reciprocity. The animal behaviors that seemed to follow the "golden rule" are actually selfish in the evolutionary sense. Instances of nepotism, manipulation, or reciprocity could no longer serve as examples of nature's inherent goodness, since such behaviors come to help maximize the inclusive fitness of the generous animal. Thus, seemingly benign, neutral, or selfless behaviors, such as sharing food with relatives, are no less selfish adaptations than the predatory bat's use of a frog's mating call to locate frog prey. Individual reproductive "selfishness" became paradigmatic in evolutionary science. Though Williams, Hamilton, and Trivers did not seek to make a big splash outside their fields, their work was influential and propelled evolutionary theory forward. Many of us have by now heard of the "selfish gene" from Richard Dawkins' 1976 book of the same name.

The shift this work represents implies not a morally neutral nature, one from which romanticized "noble savage" stories were more easily and

frequently extracted earlier in the century, or from which one could claim
the inevitability of communalism or socialism, but a sometimes morally
repugnant nature. It became increasingly clear that what spiders and birds
and orangutans do with and to one another is morally disagreeable. As
Williams puts it, "If the enemy (i.e., the cosmic process) is worse than Huxley thought, the more urgent is the need for biological understanding."[31]
Arguments like this over the past few decades pushed issues of morality
in the Darwinian context back to the surface. Many contemporary HBE
scholars and their enthusiasts began to assert that evolutionary science, far
from being morally threatening, promises to solve the values crisis.

Darwin's Soldiers: A Salvation Army

In Darwin's time, science seemed to offer standards of evidence in place of
simple faith, and Enlightenment science suggested that rational thought
and scientific reasoning would guide us toward moral and social progress.
Science, thus, became a grand narrative promising progress. For many
contemporary Darwinists, evolutionary theory's account of human origins and human nature offers meaning, purpose, and a foundation for values. Indeed, science has become a religion. If religion is "one of the chief
value-generating institutions and... also provides an overarching system
of meaning to support its values," as Philip Hefner notes, then "evolutionism can be seen as a religion."[32] The view that science can offer objective
revelations that we can use to answer questions about right and wrong or
about the meaning of life amounts to a scientific fundamentalism.

Not all HBE scholars are scientific fundamentalists. Some do not
even concern themselves with the practical/popular application of their
scholarship. Others are scientific pragmatists, seeing science as the best
method to use as the foundation upon which to establish a lasting code
of ethics. E. O. Wilson states that religions may now be replaced by "the
evolutionary epic" as "probably the best myth we will ever have."[33] The
philosopher Michael Ruse, an HBE enthusiast who has been writing for
years on evolution and its relationship to ethics, explains the implication
of contemporary evolutionary theory: "We humans are modified monkeys, not the favored creation of a benevolent God, on the sixth day. The
time has come, therefore, to face squarely our animal nature, particularly
as we interact with others."[34]

Many of today's HBE scholars are offering a religious sort of science not because they are Christians who insist that God designed the

evolutionary process, but because they proselytize with the conviction that knowledge of our evolved tendencies is the truth that will set us free. Wilson preaches a "scientific humanism" with which we can gain the knowledge of human nature necessary to overcome the challenges of our times.[35] Humanist science treats science as a source of legitimacy and guidance. HBE theorists present reason as a route to will power, self-control, and the transcendence of sexual passions.

HBE theorists who are engaged with ethical issues feel we have a crisis due to the loss of a shared, transcendent foundation for values. The loss of a shared construction of reality is certainly more pronounced today than in Darwin's day. Ralph Wendell Burhoe, founder of *Zygon: Journal of Religion and Science*, feels that the themes of Darwinism and ethics provide a means to deal with anxiety in contemporary Western culture, noting,

> The disintegration of personal meaning and of loyalties to the social order, which presently is so observable in today's world and so conspicuous in literature and the arts, should be a warning that something is disastrously wrong in today's societies.[36]

Will Durant experiences the academy as similarly chaotic; he writes, "We suffocate with uncoordinated facts; our minds are overwhelmed with sciences breeding and multiplying into specialistic chaos for want of synthetic thought and a unifying philosophy."[37]

Wilson, notes William Rottschaefer, believes that we should use our "best cognitive tool, science, in the solution of our contemporary crisis in values."[38] He hopes that sociobiology will "fashion a biology of ethics, which will make possible the selection of a more deeply understood and enduring code of moral values."[39] David Martinsen and William Rottschaefer use Wilson's argument approvingly that "we must use scientifically based reason to solve the values dilemma created by the loss of a transcendent foundation for values," and suggest that we embrace "Wilson's attempt to bridge the gap between fact and value using empirical reason," gaining from it "ultimate ethical principles."[40] The scientific method is seen as appropriate for investigating ethical problems and for laying the foundations for ethics. Evolutionary ethics is a project of gleaning ethical meaning from the study of evolution.

Wilson has articulated three "cardinal values" that sociobiology can discover and account for. These are the maintenance and preservation of the human gene pool, the maintenance of the diversity of the human gene pool, and universal human rights. These support various secondary values, which in turn provide a link to more concrete norms.[41] According to Rottschaefer, extracting normative conclusions from evolution goes like this: "What is good, right, or to be valued morally [is] that which is in harmony with, sustains, or enhances the orderly design of evolving nature including its human apex."[42] This contemporary sect of evolutionism preserves the principal value of man's progression up the proverbial evolutionary ladder.

Natural selection is an indifferent God, and human nature—the hodgepodge of adaptations we've inherited—our secular soul. HBE thought might remind us that, despite the moral horrors of the evolutionary process, "we are all special genotypically."[43] We are also immortal in an evolutionary sense. At the very least, our genes are immortal, even if humans must accept being, as David Barash puts it, "temporary, skin-encapsulated egos, serving as complex tools by means of which their potentially immortal genes replicate themselves."[44] Dawkins imparts the immortality of the gene this way:

> [I]t does not grow senile; it is no more likely to die when it is a million years old than when it is only a hundred. It leaps from body to body down the generations, manipulating body after body in its own way and for its own ends, abandoning a succession of mortal bodies before they sink in senility and death.
>
> The genes are the immortals... .[45]

Such a framing of evolution offers meaning and moral purpose, and promises the self-knowledge and self-control necessary for moral striving.

The Scientific Truth that Will Set Us Free

Admitting that genes are selfish does not mean accepting a biologically determined fate, for evolutionary apostles have paved a rather elegant path to salvation. Genes are the devil: tempting us, perhaps, if we are not careful; but we do have free will. Indeed, we can overcome our biological original sin by gaining an intellectual perspective on the evolutionary forces that lean on us; the future of our planet may very well depend on our doing so. Dawkins speaks of "turning against" our "creator genes," urging us to "rebel against the tyranny of the selfish replicators."[46] Moral striving, then, is actually the "ultimate negation of the commandment of natural selection."[47] Transcendence of human nature is the evolutionists' credo.

Williams explains how we can realize and then transcend some of our more evil tendencies:

> There is no conceivable justification for any personal concern with the interests (long-term average proliferation) of the genes we received in the lottery of meiosis and fertilization. As Huxley was the first to recognize, there is every reason to rebel against any tendency to serve such interest.[48]

Those who are not engaged in an evolutionary ethics project and are not interested in providing society with a code of ethics or turning nature into a personal religion nevertheless believe that the HBE theory gives the self-knowledge necessary for human liberation. Even the way these scholars articulate our free will has a pious character. For example, as David Buss, in *The Evolution of Desire*, explains,

> Much of what I discovered about human mating is not nice… . But a scientist cannot wish away unpleasant findings. Ultimately, the disturbing side of human mating must be confronted if its harsh consequences are ever to be ameliorated.[49]

Jared Diamond, physiologist and Pulitzer Prize-winning author of *Guns, Germs and Steel*, wrote *Why is Sex Fun? The Evolution of Human Sexuality* to tell a lay audience about the biological bases for (among other things) the battle of the sexes. If the title alone fails to make obvious that this book was intended for a wide audience, I should add that it is published by a trade press and contains absolutely no citations, footnotes, or scholarly references. In the book's preface, Diamond makes clear his faith in our ability to curb our innate tendencies once we become conscious of them:

> [T]his book may help you understand why your body feels the way it does, and why your beloved is behaving the way he or she is. Perhaps, too, if you understand why you feel driven to some self-destructive sexual behavior, that understanding may help you to gain distance from your instincts and to deal more intelligently with them.[50]

HBE theorist Richard Alexander explains, in *Darwinism and Human Affairs*, how accepting his biological original sin has revealed the path to moral repentance:

> [T]o have discovered that I love my child, not because it shares my genes, but because I have associated with it in certain fashions, and to discover that I am likely to prefer my own child to an adopted one solely

because of my reproductive history, are realizations that have simultaneously made me more likely to adopt a child, less likely to reproduce compulsively, more likely to reflect in a calm and reasonable fashion over tensions associated with sexual competition, more tolerant of others in connection with all of these enterprises, and, I believe, more likely to maintain an enjoyable existence, tolerable to others, as well as worthwhile to myself.[51]

Thus, the disciplining of our biology is not only the essence of spiritual meaning, morality, and freedom, but also the answer to our political prayers. Randy Thornhill and Craig Palmer's *A Natural History of Rape* includes a section on implications of an evolutionary perspective on rape for rape prevention efforts.[52] The authors clearly recognize that their work has social consequences, and by discussing them they attempt to be socially responsible. The point is not to rationalize male sexual violence, but to overcome it through the self-knowledge evolutionary theory offers.

Many HBE theorists (like many of us in general) are concerned about the problems of overpopulation, war, and environmental destruction. Such scholars and enthusiasts see HBE theory as an answer. As Philip Hefner, a theology professor and the editor of *Zygon: Journal of Religion and Science*, writes,

> The age in which we now live is surely the age in which the awareness that we are indeed "evolution become aware of itself" is pressing upon us with new force and urgency. Urgency, because we see now that the future depends in an important way on our having clear awareness. If sociobiology has to do with the clarity of that awareness and if ethics has to do with proper action, then our theme of sociobiology and ethics is one of the most critical themes we could possibly choose for reflection.[53]

Knowledge is the great emancipator; understanding the evolutionary origins of human evil can help us more consciously direct our evolution. This is precisely what makes these scientists think they are protected from charges of biological determinism. As Alexander explains, "Evolutionary biology is our best hope for knowing how to achieve whatever social or ethical goals we may set for ourselves."[54]

The future sustainability of the planet's ecosystems, HBE theorists believe, may depend on our becoming aware of and controlling our evolved tendencies, which in our novel, high-tech environment have spun out of control. University of Michigan HBE scholar Bobbi Low remarks,

If, as many scholars agree, current trajectories of population growth and resource consumption continue, few of the likely outcomes are pleasant. Darwin's 'Hostile Forces' are virtually identical to the Four Horseman of the Apocalypse. We live in an evolutionarily novel world that we have created: can we manage it?[55]

To her credit, Low does not have a grand solution, admitting that our strategies, whether evolutionarily informed or not, might not be effective enough. About two decades earlier, Alexander wrote that one of the primary reasons for relating human attributes to our evolutionary history "is the immense potential for self-understanding to further the interests of humanity in general—indeed, even literally to enable its survival."[56] The fall from the environment of evolutionary adaptedness was humanity's fall from grace, putting us on a path to extinction by exaggerating survival strategies more appropriate for small-scale hunting-and-gathering social organization. The apocalyptic myth is human extinction. A salvation army of Darwin's soldiers offers us knowledge of human nature, a scientific truth that will set us free.

Since personal and collective salvation is a goal of contemporary HBE theorizing, some admittedly preach in a way particularly appropriate for making converts. Clearly, the field's ambitions are far from modest. John Tooby and Leda Cosmides, and E. O. Wilson, suggest that HBE is the answer to fragmented disciplines all studying human behavior.[57] HBE can become the unifying science synthesizing approaches to human behavior.

HBE scholarship, with help from its popularizers, manipulates the misplaced Enlightenment hope that people have about discovering who they are and why we're here. HBE scholarship can't actually tell us that much about why we feel or behave as we do, and how we should expect others to behave, but the Judeo–Christian myths in HBE perform that work of manipulating our hopes. HBE scientists and their popularizers, like so many people in Western cultures today, are humanistic in their understanding of science, progress, and politics. This helps explain the popularity of evolutionary answers to questions about everyday life and morality.

Moral Answers for the Moral Animal

The Darwinian moral answer to our prayers is spread widely by HBE enthusiasts who write books for general audiences. Robert Wright's best-selling book *The Moral Animal: Evolutionary Psychology and Everyday Life*

illustrates the idea of biological original sin.[58] Wright tells us that everything bad or good that we do is an expression of our genes' selfish interests
in reproducing. It's just that we have evolved to deceive ourselves about
it. Wright, a writer and magazine editor, is an HBE enthusiast and, as
such, exercises less restraint than scientists usually do. He invites readers
to consider the benefits, and the fun, of applying evolutionary psychology
to common questions about marriage and fidelity. One lesson about marriage, for example, is that "lasting love is something a person has to decide
to experience. Lifelong monogamous devotion is just not natural—not for
women, even, and emphatically not for men. It requires what, for lack of
a better term, we can call an act of will."[59] This is because, Wright asserts,
"The male mind is the largest single obstacle to lifelong monogamy—
and certainly the largest such obstacle that emerges distinctly from the
new Darwinian paradigm."[60] With evolutionary insight, HBE enthusiasts
faithfully insist, comes moral capacity.

John Beckstrom's *Darwinism Applied* explains to a broad audience the
role evolutionary theory can have in social affairs. Beckstrom, also the author
of *Sociobiology in the Law* and *Evolutionary Jurisprudence*, argues that

> evolutionary science cannot be used 'normatively'—it cannot be used to
> determine what social goals ought to be pursued. But once social plan-
> ners, public or private, have used their values and tastes to select social
> goals, modern evolutionary science may then step in to provide factual
> guides toward achieving those goals—facilitative guides.[61]

The goal of Beckstrom's book is clearly stated:

> I want to introduce people who have social goals to a modern, rapidly
> developing aspect of evolutionary science that could help to achieve
> many of those goals. This evolutionary perspective ... deals with the
> evolved biological basis for social behavior in all organisms including
> humans.[62]

In explaining that evolutionary theory neither can nor should define
political goals, Beckstrom thinks he's immune to charges of Social Darwinism, which a century ago not only said how to achieve a goal, but assumed
what that goal was (namely, unrestrained competition and survival of the
fittest). What he thinks made Social Darwinism bad was not the status of
evolutionary theory as objective science, but the scientists who were not
distanced enough in the process of determining social goals.

Beckstrom thus chooses goals he regards as noncontroversial—the reduction of rape, child abuse, incest, and war—to show how evolutionary learning can help us achieve these goals. That people disagree over what counts as rape and child abuse seem not to bother Beckstrom. Should a husband have unrestricted sexual rights with his own wife, or is it rape if she isn't willing? Can an individual under 18 consent to sex with someone over 18? The categories for all these social ills are contested. Words like *abuse, justice, health*, and *diversity* are terms all people agree on until they have to define them. Beckstrom treats ethics as simplistically as he does science while he works to establish the two as distinct, but complementary, realms. As I will address in more detail in chapter 5, whether we're talking about scientific claims, political goals, or the application of science to political goals, no uncontestable underlying foundation exists upon which to ground our position.

Notably, Beckstrom acknowledges the lack of agreement over how to define what constitutes "child abuse" in the beginning of his second chapter, but then, with arrogant aplomb, simply decides to use "a sociobiological definition" of it, saying that child abuse is conduct likely to decrease the child's fitness;[63] so much for his argument that evolutionary thinking can't define the social problems, but can only present us with solutions. He does not go over any competing definitions of rape. He insists that increasing the criminal penalty for rape, and advertising that penalty widely, would deter rape because

> when men confront a reproductive strategy option, their behavioral mechanisms will 'compute' whether the possible benefits of pursuing the option are worth the costs of it in view of other options that may or may not be available for pursuing the 'inclusive fitness' goal.[64]

Of course, such reasoning does not even take into account the problem men have of recognizing what is or is not rape; consequently, they may not expect punishment and may even feel vastly importuned if they are resisted physically, arrested, or otherwise punished. Beckstrom again keeps his distance—after all, he doesn't want to compromise his putative objectivity by acting as if he were concerned about reducing rape or increasing women's freedom. Thus, before he goes over the various ways for increasing state retribution for rape, he writes,

> Nothing said hereafter is meant to be a prescription for what ought to be done about rape. I intend merely to survey feasible means of increasing

male perceptions of retribution on the assumption that a society might want to pursue that route. We should keep in mind that a penalty might be quite effective as a deterrent, yet undesirable.[65]

With a robust commitment to the scientific view of individuals, neither contemporary HBE theorists nor their enthusiasts fear, as did many a century before them, that what is said about human nature will negatively influence how people act. Instead, as Beckstrom puts it,

> [L]arge leaps forward in evolutionary learning in the last few decades of the twentieth century have brought us to the beginning of an era where science may be able to offer social planners advice on how to reduce or even eliminate a large array of social problems.[66]

The historical transition from an understanding of human nature that is threatening to destroy all morality, as in Darwin's day, to a nature that is manageable could only have been achieved with the rise of science as the basis for true knowledge about human nature. HBE theorists see people as having a nature and cultural patterns as expressing that nature. Consequently, avoiding that nature will only perpetuate social problems—our natural tendencies will control us if we don't understand and control them.

Daniel Dennett, a professor of philosophy and the co-director of the Tufts University Center for Cognitive Studies, wrote *Darwin's Dangerous Idea* to highlight the importance of Darwinian thinking. Still defensive about creationists and others who reject Darwinism for fear that it robs us of moral foundations or is antireligious or politically incorrect, referring to "those who want to dig a moat separating us from most if not all of the dreadful implications they think they see in Darwinism,"[67] HBE enthusiasts like Dennett insist that Darwinism can give us meaning and provide a moral foundation. In *Darwin's Dangerous Idea*, Dennett explains, "My admiration for Darwin's magnificent idea is unbounded, but I, too, cherish many of the ideas and ideals that it *seems* to challenge, and want to protect them."[68] Dennett does not go so far as to suggest that Darwinism can provide a neat formula for right and wrong. But he does argue that ethics on an evolutionary foundation is an even stronger ethics; his sense of wonder and meaning have withstood the test of scientific scrutiny.

Science and Certainty

According to social theorist Anthony Giddens, modernity has revealed uncertainty and doubt rather than the certainty that once seemed to be its promise.[69] Late modernity places the epistemological assumptions of the Enlightenment in question. Some have welcomed the loss of certainty that has come with questioning Enlightenment science; others are terribly anxious about it and are still trying to make science into a system of certainty rather than doubt. Extracting moral meaning or ethical prescriptions from evolution can be seen as a response to the contingency presented by evolutionary theory itself. Indeed, the theory of evolution seems to symbolize those anxieties characteristic of modernity: contingency, an amoral universe, the lack of a universal foundation for ethical principles or political action, and nihilism.

As many scholars have noted, science enjoys a remarkable popularity in our culture. John Michael, author of *Anxious Intellects*, notes that science enjoys this authority in part due to our yearning for stabilized truth. The popularity of physicist Stephen Hawking, Michael posits, "rests on an ambivalent popular identification of science with utopian aspirations, of scientists as the last intellectuals who might manage to bespeak universal laws and therefore free us from contingency, from chance, from history, from politics."[70]

Many HBE theorists carry out a long tradition of using their scientific work to speak to questions about human affairs and social problems.[71] Wilson is most famous in the HBE context for such efforts in his *On Human Nature* and *Consilience*. Many scientists outside of HBE theory have taken on this role as well. For example, the physicist Fritjof Capra, author of the best-seller *The Tao of Physics*, draws parallels between Eastern mysticism and modern physics. Likewise, Stephen Hawking's popular work has a philosophical and religious status among many readers. And, of course, Albert Einstein's comment that "you cannot simultaneously prepare for and prevent war" is repeated on posters, T-shirts, and bumper stickers everywhere. Seeing science as an institution that can resolve messy political disputes over how people should act and what a good society would look like enables science to become our new Bible.

Since scientific knowledge is popularly seen as an objective reference for social criticism, and such a reference is thought necessary for such criticism, what could be more appropriate than HBE theory's involvement with ethics, or with your average American guy gaining meaning from HBE thought? In an age of radical doubt with a lingering foundationalist tradition that sees science as promising necessary certainty, what better than Darwinism to respond to the epistemological crisis of the breakdown in Christian cosmology? It seems only fitting that Darwinian science has become the Second Coming.

The theory that over a century ago so sharply provoked anxiety over morality is now offered as a scientific fundamentalist cure. Such a scientific fundamentalism, however, is not the only way to respond to the uncertainty of the modern age and the breakdown of religious and other traditions. Many scholars have found new ways to think about knowledge and politics, eschewing the search for certainty. These scholars, connected loosely under such labels as *postmodern*, *poststructuralist*, *feminist*, and *postcolonial*, have expressed skepticism about the need for moral absolutes and argue that attempts to produce an ultimate, universalizable truth are authoritarian.[72] They have also insisted that, though science may very well be socially beneficial, it is not neutral—and so its usefulness is not due to some presumed neutrality. Science is not pure, and reason used to promote social or moral progress masks the values and interests projected under its guise.[73]

Foundationalism assumes the need for, and existence of, one authoritative framework for distinguishing the right from the wrong, the real from the unreal, and the healthy from the sick. While appealing to a (however illusory) neutral, absolutist foundation does make possible the authoritative arbitration of social conflicts and justification of political arrangements, it is precisely this universalizing tendency that reproduces the ability of those who already have privileged access to knowledge making to determine the normative framework with any credibility. It is not that evolution provides a bad foundation, but that foundationalism itself is troubling. It sets up a way to make politics invisible in the knowledge production process. Invoking God's will, or nature's, hides the political context in which such a will was "revealed" or "discovered," the interests of those who deem it important, and the dissent of those who are unwillingly held accountable to it.

The easiest way for HBE scholars to deflect criticism is to assume that the critic is simply afraid of the implications for ethics of the HBE argument. HBE scholars will remind themselves and their readership that evolutionary theory has always been resisted by some because of its putative implication of atheism and ethical chaos. Indeed, HBE theorists fixate on resistance to their presentation of a nonreligious and, therefore, uncomfortable view of humanity. For example, HBE scholar Bobbi Low speaks to a religious audience she imagines reading her book.

No doubt, some religious people still resist the claims of evolutionary scientists. But, as chapter 3 elaborates, many men have no problem seeing themselves in evolutionary terms. In fact, for many men, evolutionary ideas offer quite a comfortable view of manhood. Given that a significant number of men see evolutionary theory not as threatening, but as a way of making sense of themselves in a scientific, foundationalist culture, it seems fair to say that a caveman identity marks the resurrection of evolutionary theory as a moral system for men.

The Caveman as Resurrection

How does the historical transition from the rejection to the acceptance of Darwinian thought fit into patterns of manhood in the West? Why did men in the 1800s find solace in the demand for civility, while today so many resist the demand to be civil by embracing a caveman ethos to prove they can't be tamed? According to gender studies scholars Susan Bordo and Michael Kimmel, the fear of the "sissification" of boys in an industrializing America gave rise to a new passion for organized sport, male-only activities like Boy Scouts and meat eating.[74] Men even drank tonics they thought would put hair on their chests. The most privileged of men began to cultivate what they thought was their animal nature. (A recent version of this was the Wild Man movement of the late 1980s and early 1990s.) To be an untamed caveman is now to be a potent heterosexual guy.

Darwinism eventually turned into a new Adam and Eve story by which nature, rather than God, intended men and women for one another. The religious order of mating turned into a natural order of mating. And man became not a civilized gentleman but a passionate ape, augmenting a new masculinity, which I call *Homo resurrectus*. *Homo resurrectus* is the scientism of Darwin's day and the resurrection of evolutionary theory as the answer to a moral crisis most sharply felt by men.

Enlightenment science moved sex away from sin, but left us with complicated political arguments about regulating sex. HBE theorists are the latest in a barrage of scholars who have tried to reveal human sexual nature. Two hundred years ago, our bodily desires would not have made us who we are. Today science describes our bodily desires and allows us to craft our identities around them. HBE scholarship fits in neatly here, offering an account of what is simultaneously natural and normal. Michel Foucault has pointed out that sexuality has been regulated not through laws or censoring, but through ideas about what is a healthy sexuality and who is a normal sexual person leading a normal and healthy sex life. Many scientific approaches to sexuality have emerged, including those of medicine, psychoanalysis, demography, and sexology. Of course, HBE theorists do not say, "This is right." However, in the social context of scientism—the gleaning of values from science or a scientific theory—it should be no surprise that people take up HBE ideas as a way to regulate their lives, desires, and social relationships.[75]

Given the emergence of science, and evolution in particular, as a grand narrative used both to understand people and to determine what is morally correct, it should be no surprise that evolutionary arguments interest, if not guide, a lot of people, even (or perhaps especially) those who are not scientists. Nor should it be surprising, in light of the many public and private discussions about the problems of men, that evolutionary stories about men specifically have circulated widely in our culture.

While all men can now embrace a caveman identity, it is still men of color—particularly African American and Latino men—who are at risk of being judged, jailed, or otherwise punished for having this putative instinct for aggression. In other words, all guys are culturally encouraged to see themselves as cavemen; however, we do live in a racially stratified society. Consequently, men of color still risk being more negatively understood and treated for any cavemanesque behaviors.

To be sure, Darwin's theory created a new Adam *and* a new Eve. But HBE theory is far more often presented as an answer about men than about women. Women figure in the discourse about cavemen as the passive objects of cavemen's desires and actions. Women are the wives men want to forsake for a younger woman, the ones with the signals of fertility men recognize and compete over, the "girls" who men ogle or rape, and the coworkers who get sexually harassed.

Evolutionary discourse about women, then, has not circulated in popular culture the way evolutionary discourse about men has. But it is sometimes taken up by small groups. For instance, breast-feeding advocates commonly employ evolutionary rhetoric to convince women that breast-feeding their infants is better than bottle feeding, since that's how evolution designed us.[76] In such cases, evolution is invoked specifically to justify a positive practice. So, when HBE theory is invoked about women, it is quite explicitly prescriptive: this is natural and should be done today. When stories about the caveman and his needs, problems, and cravings travel through popular culture, they are often descriptive rather than prescriptive ("Hey, we're just explaining that you desire to cheat on your wife, but you don't have to do it"). But, of course, this "you don't have to do it" caveat is given in a culture that tends to insist that we have a sexuality that must be asserted, affirmed, liberated, and fulfilled. Such a caveat, then, will likely fall on deaf ears.

Since the voice of science has replaced the word of God, it is no wonder that people take up HBE ideas about men with great enthusiasm, gaining moral meaning and self-identity from them. The next chapter explores the ways in which evolutionary narratives of men's behaviors and desires have become increasingly popular accounts circulating throughout American culture. In that chapter, I also offer an explanation of just how such narratives could find their way into men's lived experiences of who they are.

3

HOMO HABITUS

EVOLUTION, POPULAR CULTURE, AND THE EMBODIED ETHOS OF MALE SEXUALITY

The Caveman in Popular Culture

Most of us can call up some image of prehistoric man and his treatment of women. He's a shaggy, well-muscled caveman whose name is Thor, and we might picture him, club in hand, approaching a scrawny but curvaceous woman whom he bangs over the head and drags by the hair into a cave to mate. (If she protests, her resistance is futile.) I'd be willing to bet that the majority of readers recognize that imagery. Indeed, today an image of modern men as guided by such prehistoric tendencies is even celebrated on T-shirts sold on Web sites that allow people to post and sell their own designs. One such image for sale at the cafepress.com Web site portrays a version of Thor, wearing a fur pelt and walking with club in hand, accompanied by the slogan "ME FIND WOMAN!" Another image available for T-shirts, boxer shorts, baseball caps, and coffee mugs features a man dressed in a one-shoulder fur pelt, club in hand, behind a cavewoman in a fur bikini outfit who is cooking a skinned animal on a spit, with the saying "MENS PRIORITYS [sic]: 10,000 YEARS LATER AND STILL ON THE HUNT FOR FOOD AND SEX!" Another image features only the club, with the saying, "caveman: primitive pimpin'." (Of course,

Mens Prioritys [sic].

here "pimping" does not mean finding customers for prostitutes but rather, as popularized by hip-hop culture, having lots of women, nice cars, and "bling-bling" jewelry.)

It's not hard to imagine some of the most clean-shaven, well groomed, shirt-and-tie guys who ogle a woman thinking, mid-ogle, that this is natural, and indeed based in human evolution. What excites them and how they explain that excitement can be traced to ideas about evolution. Evolutionary explanations have become part of popular consciousness. The New York man who sexually assaulted a woman while declaring, "Welcome back to the caveman times" (see the introduction to this volume) invoked an evolutionary narrative. "The caveman times" is an imagined era of total male supremacy and virility. Never mind that cavemen did not necessarily rule cavewomen—all cartoonish images of cavemen clubbing cavewomen over the head aside. The caveman mystique is a vision of male physical and

Primitive Pimpin'.

social power over women, of male efficaciousness, male confidence, male strength, male pride, and male power. Pop culture celebrates male heterosexuality as irrepressible and pop-Darwinism is its method.

Popular culture is a political Petri dish for Darwinian ideas about sex. As such, it is worth examining—even when magazine writers and television producers intentionally "dumb down" relatively sophisticated academic claims. Average American guys don't read academic evolutionary science, but many do read about science in popular magazines and in best-selling books about the significance of the latest scientific ideas.

This chapter examines some of the stories about cavemen circulating in our culture and argues that they shape men's experience of their bodies. Using Pierre Bourdeau's theory of *habitus*, or his account of how cultural ideas are taken up in the form of bodily habits and tastes that reinforce behavioral norms and social inequality, this chapter shows how scientific theories find their way into both popular culture and men's corporeal habits and attitudes. In so doing, it demonstrates how evolution has become popular culture, where popular culture is more than just media representations, but refers to the institutions of everyday life: family, marriage, school, work—all sites where gender and racial knowledges are performed according to images people have available to them in actionable repertoires, scripts, and narratives. As popular culture, evolutionary narratives offer men a way to embody male sexuality. *Homo habitus* represents the contribution of contemporary evolutionary science to an embodied caveman ethos.

In their book chronicling the pervasive iconography of the gene in popular culture, Dorothy Nelkin and Susan Lindee explain that popular culture provides "narratives of meaning."[1] Those narratives filter complex ideas, provide guidance, and influence how people see themselves and evaluate other people, ideas, and policies. In this way, Nelkin and Lindee argue, DNA works as an ideology to justify boundaries of identity and legal rights, as well as to explain criminality, addiction, and personality. Of course, addict genes and criminal genes are misnomers—the definitions of what counts as an addict and what counts as a crime have shifted throughout history. Understanding DNA stories as ideological clarifies why, for example, people made sense of Elvis Presley's talents and shortcomings by referring to his genetic stock.[2] To call narratives of DNA ideological, then, is *not* to resist the scientific argument that deoxyribonucleic acid is a double helix structure carrying information forming living cells and tissues, but to look at the way people make sense of DNA and use DNA to make sense of people and events in their daily lives.

In parallel fashion, I look here at the way some popular texts make sense of evolutionary claims about men. I call the circulation of a caveman discourse in popular culture a *mystique* because, as I argue later in the book, this air of powerful, virile masculinity is not natural and ultimately not fulfilling. I pay special attention to the ways in which the caveman ideology, much of which centers on men's aggressive heterosexuality, gets embodied and thereby reproduced.

Caveman Therapy

Contemporary sexual and gender identities are increasingly wrapped up in a popular Darwinian discourse. For instance, an article in *Men's Fitness* magazine uses the man-the-hunter story to excuse men's inexpressiveness.[3]

Men originally went off together, away from women, to strategize about hunting, and this process evidently requires little emotional expression, which is why women today can expect men to withdraw from rather than talk with them during a conflict. Further, the article explains, men's contemporary social positions—themselves presumably extensions of manly hunting careers—demand being out of touch with one's feelings. The article asks readers, rhetorically, to imagine what being in touch with one's feelings would be like while attending to people in an emergency room or building a skyscraper. Thus, we are told, "If you trace male behavior back 40,000 years to the cave, it's easier to see why men are the way they are."[4]

Evolution is commonly invoked to explain many aspects of men's pain and problems, presumably to elicit women's empathy and men's self-understanding. In an interview for a public television series, the figurehead of the mythopoetic men's movement, Robert Bly, invokes the evolutionary narrative of man the hunter to explain male violence and grief. This presumably primeval role has influenced the male "collective unconscious." Male grief is thus caused by men's evolutionary past, as Bly has put it, "when men were asked to be violent" (the assumption being that the necessity to kill animals to survive causes grief).[5] So compelling is the evolutionary myth of man as hunter that the obvious fact that Americans slaughter countless animals today without hunting and without apparent grief is erased. Bly also presumes that men have a warrior instinct that must be properly channeled, lest it lead to gang violence, wife beating, and the like.[6]

John Gray's best-selling *Men Are from Mars, Women Are from Venus* also assumes male–female differences and suggests that men need "a cave."[7] This cave of one's own (a basement room, den, or garage) is a place to which a man can retreat during a conflict with a woman. Warren Farrell's book about gender relations, *Why Men Are the Way They Are* (which comes from a men's rights perspective),[8] argues that men's primary fantasy is to have intercourse with as many women as possible without making a commitment to them or their children. He argues that women's primary fantasy is to secure a monogamous relationship with one wealthy man.

Other counseling approaches and workshops about relationships rely on this logic as well. For example, Ron Smotherman's 1980s Empowering Man/Woman Relationship Training workshop also takes as its founding assumption that evolution made men and women different, and that understanding this is a key to learning how to get along with one another in heterosexual relationships. Smotherman insists that women and men would do well to realize that men are constantly trying to prove that they are bigger, stronger, smarter, and faster than other men. This primal need to establish oneself in some sort of dominance hierarchy informs many, if not all, of men's social interactions. The relationship workshop even shows clips from the movie about our evolutionary ancestors, *Quest for Fire*,[9] to encourage the participants to understand the roots of these sex differences.

The humorous self-help book by two male authors going in disguise as Smith and Doe, *What Men Don't Want Women to Know: The Secrets, the Lies, the Unspoken Truth*, bills itself as "the book men pray women won't read."[10] Beginning with the basic principle that "man is a sexual animal," this book tells women that "if men could get away with it, they would buy and sell women like slaves."[11] Smith and Doe humorously expose men's bad-boy behaviors and desires, reasoning that to be forewarned is to be forearmed. They caution women that "your man is in a dangerous environment when he's at work, and thus you must heed the following warning: IF HE HAS *ANY* ATTRACTIVE UNDERLINGS, BE WARNED!"[12] Their story is that men are this way naturally:

> All we are saying is, man is a sexual animal. But unlike an animal, he has a mind that can reason, lie, and, worst for you, *FANTASIZE*... The primitive nature of every man is the innate desire to *bed every woman* who even *marginally* turns him on.[13]

Finally, they generalize about men's sexual needs:

> Don't ever forget what your man tells you he wants, and don't ever stop giving it to him, or he will surely fulfill his desires with a more willing participant. (*Smith and Doe guarantee the above* or you may return the unused portion of this book for a full refund!) How can men *need* something sexual to stay fulfilled? Why can't they curb their urges like any other civilized human? Because, besides being uncivilized, men's sexual needs are infinitely stronger than those of the most addicted drug addict on earth.[14]

Silly books like Smith and Doe's must be understood alongside the academic discourse about evolution and male sexuality because those academic ideas are taken up in a broader social context. My own book search at amazon.com provides an example of the academic–pop culture connection. When I looked up human behavior and evolution (HBE) scholar Robin Baker's *Sperm Wars*, the online bookstore immediately provided me with a list of other books I might like to buy, which included a series of nonscholarly books on how to pick up women and a book called *The Way of the Superior Man*.

Randy Thornhill and Craig Palmer's *A Natural History of Rape* is an academic HBE book, but was also a big hit reaching far beyond academic circles.[15] The book was heavily promoted by the MIT Press and was reviewed and debated in almost all major newspapers. Even before the book was published, the authors had published "Why Men Rape" in *The Sciences*, a journal published by the New York Academy of Sciences, and news outlets had over 50 reports on their theory that rape—even in human beings—can be understood through the lens of evolutionary psychology as an adaptation. The book received a review in a place most authors only dream about: the Sunday *New York Times*. Later, Thornhill and Palmer appeared on CNN's *Talkback Live*, NBC's *Today Show*, CBS's *Early Show,* and NPR's *Talk of the Nation*.[16] The amazing amount of media coverage of the book was complemented by numerous Web sites addressing the book's conclusions. The MIT Press' first print-run of 10,000 books sold out in less than a month.[17] While that may not sound like a lot to Stephen King, most academics never hope to sell anywhere close to a total of 10,000 book copies.

Thornhill and Palmer position their theory in opposition to the reigning social science view of rape. They see their policy solutions—such as having the state teach boys, before they get their drivers' licenses, about their biological propensity and teach girls not to incite that propensity with provocative clothing—as superior because their theory of why rape occurs is scientific. It's tempting to get sidetracked by the shortcomings of such a policy solution,[18] but the point of this chapter is to establish that the evolution of men's aggressive heterosexuality is a discourse circulating widely in our culture. Besides, many popular feminist writers immediately gave the book plenty of outraged attention. Indeed, a familiar face-off occurred in the media: feminists are ideological and emotional about rape; scientists are objective. Thus, *A Natural History of Rape* enabled men, most of whom are far more likely to identify with the still largely male field of science than with feminism, to understand themselves as sexually aggressive cavemen. The attention this book received was complemented by an almost decade-long climate of popular attention to evolutionary perspectives on male sexuality.

As chapter 2 revealed, plenty of pro-Darwin propaganda emerged in the late 1800s and early 1900s. Today's Darwinian propaganda focuses attention on sexuality, male–female relationships, and men's predatory, lustful sexual energy as it is directed at women with particular physical features. Popular magazines tell men that they have a biological propensity to favor women with the faces of 11-year-old girls (where the eyes and chin are close together) and a waist-to-hip ratio of .7 (where the waist measures 70 percent that of the hips). Men are told that their sexist double standard concerning appearance is evolutionary. Some of this research is very speculative—for instance, in some studies, men are simply shown photos of women with specific waist-to-hip ratios and then asked, "Would you like to spend the rest of your life with this woman?"—as though such staged answers reveal something about the individuals' real-life choices. But the results of this research make great copy.

Men's Health magazine in 1999 offered an article called "The Mysteries of Sex … Explained!" and relies on evolutionary theory, quoting several professors in the field, to explain "why most women won't sleep with you." The article elucidates,

> Stop blaming your wife. The fault lies with Mother Nature, the pit boss of procreation. Neil M. Malamuth, Ph.D., professor of psychology at UCLA, explains. "You're in Las Vegas with 10 grand. Your gambling strategy will depend on which form your money takes. With 10 chips worth $1,000 each, you'd weigh each decision cautiously. With 10,000 $1 chips, you'd throw them around." That's reproductive strategy in a nutshell.[19]

Popular magazine articles like this follow a standard formula. They quote the scientists, reporting on the evolutionary theorists' research, and offer funny anecdotes about male sexuality to illustrate the research findings. This *Men's Health* article continues to account for men's having fetishes:

> Men are highly sexed creatures, less interested in relationship but highly hooked on visuals, says David Givens, Ph.D., an anthropologist. "Because sex carries fewer consequences for men, it's easier for us to use objects as surrogate sexual partners." Me? I've got my eye on a Zenith, model 39990.[20]

Time magazine's 1994 cover story "Our Cheating Hearts" reports that "the emerging field known as evolutionary psychology" gives us "fresh detail about the feelings and thoughts that draw us into marriage—or push us out."[21] After explaining the basics about men being less discriminating about their sexual partners than women, the article moves on to discuss why people divorce, anticipating resistance to the evolutionary explanation:

> Objections to this sort of analysis are predictable: "But people leave marriages for emotional reasons. They don't add up their offspring and pull out their calculators." But emotions are just evolution's executioners. Beneath the thoughts and feelings and temperamental differences marriage counselors spend their time sensitively assessing are the stratagems of the genes—cold, hard equations composed of simple variables: social status, age of spouse, number of children, their ages, outside romantic opportunities and so on. Is the wife really duller and more nagging than she was 20 years ago? Maybe, but maybe the husband's tolerance for nagging has dropped now that she is 45 and has no reproductive future.[22]

In case *Time* readers react to the new evolutionary psychology as part of a plot to destroy the cherished nuclear family, they are told that

> progress will also depend on people using the explosive insight of evolutionary psychology in a morally responsible way.... We are potentially moral animals—which is more than any other animal can say—but we are not naturally moral animals. The first step to being moral is to realize how thoroughly we aren't.[23]

The ABC news program *Day One* reported in 1995 on evolutionary psychologist David Buss' book, *The Evolution of Desire*.[24] Buss appeared on the show, which elaborated his theory by presenting us with the supermodel Cindy Crawford and the Barbie doll, presumably as representations of what men are wired to find desirable. As Buss explained in the interview, our evolutionary forefathers who did not prefer women with high cheek bones, big eyes, lustrous hair, and full lips did not reproduce. As Buss put it, those men who happened to like someone who was older, sicker, or infertile "are not our ancestors. We are all the descendants of those men who preferred young healthy women and so as offspring, as descendants of those men, we carry with us their desires."[25]

We know that many watch such television news shows. But are average American guys paying attention to evolutionary theory? Do they get a sense of themselves and their actions from it? One clue is that on that same television show, *Penthouse* magazine publisher Bob Guccioni was interviewed and explained that men are simply biologically designed to enjoy looking at sexy women: "This may be very politically incorrect, but that's the way it is.... . It's all part of our ancestral conditioning."[26] Evolutionary narratives clearly work for publishers of pornography marketed to men.

Modern men can easily be sucked into a view of women as attractive commodities, and then rationalize their view by referring to their evolved nature. HBE scholars, along with everyday guys, observe a cultural-consumer preoccupation with sex. But this interest in and talk about sex itself has a history; it cannot naively be taken as evidence of evolutionary theories. The advertising system co-opts evolutionary discourse, and prevailing ideas of gender difference more generally, in the effort to sell commodities by producing erotically charged desires.

Newsweek's 1996 cover story "The Biology of Beauty: What Science Has Discovered About Sex Appeal" argues that the beauty lust that humans exhibit "is often better suited to the Stone Age than to the Information Age; the qualities we find alluring may be powerful emblems of health, fertility and resistance to disease.... ." Though "beauty isn't all that matters in life," the article asserts, "our weakness for 'biological quality' is the cause of endless pain and injustice."[27]

Sometimes the magazines and TV shows covering the biological basis of sexual desire give a nod to the critics. This *Newsweek* article, for instance, quotes feminist writer Katha Pollitt, who insists that "human beings cannot be reduced to DNA packets."[28] And then, as if to affirm Pollitt's claim, homosexuality is invoked as an example of the countless nonadaptive delights we desire: "Homosexuality is hard to explain as a biological adaptation. So is stamp collecting.... . We pursue countless passions that have no direct bearing on survival."[29] Thus, when there is a nod to ways in which humans are not hardwired, homosexual desires are framed as oddities having no basis in nature, while heterosexual attraction along the lines of stereotypical heterosexual male fantasy is framed as biological. Heterosexual desire enjoys a *biologically correct* status.

Caveman Edutainment

The 1993 PBS *Nature* series study *The Nature of Sex* tells us the HBE basics: that relatively little difference in size exists between human males and females, that human females have concealed ovulation, that humans have big brains and a long period of infant dependency for that brain to develop, and because of such huge sex differences in parental investment, women needed male parental investment of time and resources, and men competed against other men for sexual access to women (who are choosy).[30] Due to the fact that human males do not have assurance of paternity, they are possessive of female mates. Sweet romantic gestures like hand-holding indicate this "mate guarding."

We are shown examples of this behavior in a beach scene of young, childless, heterosexual, white people at what looks like the spring break vacation of wealthy college students. We are not shown examples of this among heavily clothed Muslims, nor are we shown a predominantly gay beach on New York's Fire Island, nor even examples among those ever-popular stars of nature shows, the Masai people of eastern Africa. We are simply supposed to take it on faith that the young, white, Western, heterosexual, childless culture of college spring break represents our ancestors' mating habits. (I half expected to see a scene of our ancestors in a spring break cave where cavewomen would lift up their animal-skin tops and show their breasts in exchange for Mardi Gras rocks.)

We are also told that since men are on average only 20 percent larger than women, ancestral men were not judged by size and strength alone, yet we cut to a scene of young men with chiseled muscles working out in a weight room. Still, it seems, generations of women who chose muscular men inspired competition among men and, hence, pushed the male body to look this way. Never mind that without workouts in a gym the male body doesn't look that way. Nor can we assume that the male body looked that way in the environment of evolutionary adaptedness (the hunting and gathering part of our human history). The female body can't look that way, the show says. Cut to a scene of women in a dance studio doing an aerobic workout, with a close-up on a woman's rear in hot pink leggings with a black leotard cutting up the sides of her butt cheeks. While telling us that these patterns have their roots in survival needs of the past, the program, like many popular portrayals of evolution and gender, glamorizes and naturalizes Western, contemporary patterns of gender differentiation.

The show does not portray men as cheaters who are always seeking new sexual opportunities. On the contrary, the show's narrator explains that, in the end, it's bonding and finding a mate that we seek, even when reproduction is impossible (cut to a scene of two men walking arm-in-arm) or when reproduction is completed (cut to scene of an elderly heterosexual couple walking arm-in-arm). This nuclear family model turns out to be quite common in pop-Darwinist depictions.

Zoologist Desmond Morris explains how evolutionary theory applies to humans in his 1999 six-part television series, *Desmond Morris' The Human Animal: A Personal View of the Human Species*. The first show in the series, "Beyond Survival," draws from his book *The Naked Ape*, explaining that humans are relatively hairless with little to protect themselves besides their big brains.[31] This is stated as we watch two naked people, one male and one female, walk through a public place where everyone else is dressed in modern-day clothing. Both are white, both are probably 25 to 30 years old, both look like models (the man with well chiseled muscles, a suntan, and no chest hair; the woman thin, yet shapely with larger than average breasts, shaved legs, and a manicured pubic region). This presentation of man and woman in today's aesthetically ideal form as the image of what all of us were once like is *de rigueur* for any popular representation of HBE ideas. No woman is flabby, flat-chested, or has body hair; no man has pimples or back hair. These culturally mandated ideal body types are presented as the image of what our human ancestors naturally looked like. In this way and others, such shows posit modern aesthetic ideals as states of nature.

The caveman comes to us not only in nonfiction public television shows, but also in popular films. The 1981 movie *Quest for Fire* (*La Guerre da feu*) centers on early humans' need to keep fire—and its advertising copy boasts of depicting not only compelling human drama, but also "realistic insights into prehistoric man."[32] It begins with a written preamble talking about our ancestors' lives 80,000 years ago and their need for fire. Adding to the "reality" element of the film is the opening credit to HBE scholar Desmond Morris, who provided the body language and gestures for the actors. But amid scene after scene of mostly men fighting animals and other people, the film also presents men surprising women from behind and copulating with them while they yelp ultimately helpless protests. The film includes one scene of face-to-face heterosexual intercourse, in which the woman turns around and shows the man how to do it. This couple ends up, near story's end, snuggling under a full moon, admiring the woman's pregnant belly. That our evolutionary history is depicted this way flies in the face of any basic understanding that women, like men, had big brains. One wonders, for instance, if such unwanted physical intrusions were part of social life why female ancestors would have ever worn clothing that left their bottoms exposed. (Hello? It's called a *loincloth*!)

Some readers may be tempted to dismiss the representations in *Quest for Fire* as tenuous masculinist ideologies that no one in their right mind would take for the reality of our evolutionary history. But that would give too much credit to many viewers. Not only did the Empowering Man/ Woman Relationship Training weekend workshop use a clip from *Quest for Fire* for consciousness-raising purposes, but a university student of mine also invoked the film when he disagreed with my feminist critique of natural male aggression rooted in the cave days. "C'mon," he protested, "I saw *Quest for Fire!*"

Iceman, a dramatic film from 1984, features a Neanderthal who comes to life when researchers melt the ice they found him in and revive him.[33] While mainly a story about the oppressiveness of being studied by the high-tech medical researchers, the film includes the iceman encountering a woman (one of the researchers), for whom, after a few sniffs and feels, he makes an offer to the male researcher—as if human male ancestors were so patriarchal that they traded women as commodities.

The 1992 Hollywood comedy *Encino Man* also features an iced-over caveman who comes to life after being unearthed and thawed out—but in this case by two male high school students in Encino, California.[34] Perhaps representing the modern young men's lost (or future) unrestrained masculine (hetero)sexuality, Encino man sniffs out and makes a beeline to seize an unacquainted young female beauty, climbing over various technological obstacles like they were trees. The film ends with the Encino man's downward spiral in contemporary California, conceivably revealing human nature to be better suited for life outdoors around a fire, where our hero eventually winds up, with his recently defrosted cavewife.

The caveman narrative reveals an entire, collective history of the development of science as an authoritative moral answer to questions of who men are and what they want. I turn now to a number of pop-Darwinist claims that have the moral purpose of liberating men from being controlled by their caveman natures. Their message: men can become enlightened cavemen.

Moral Lessons for Cavemen

A number of popular versions of man as caveman make an attempt to liberate men by getting them to see themselves differently. These versions do not tell men that they are not cavemen, but that they are cavemen with potential. They either make fun of men's putatively natural shortcomings or encourage them to cage the caveman within through a kind of scientific consciousness-raising.

Rob Becker's one-man show *Defending the Caveman* played on Broadway and elsewhere from 1993 to 2005. This performance piece poking fun at sex differences is the longest-running solo play in Broadway history. It relies on a longstanding man-as-hunter and woman-as-gatherer framework, from which modern sex differences follow. Cavemen hunted and focused on their prey until killing it. Cavewomen gathered things to use in the cave home. Men are thus strong silent types while women are into communication and togetherness. More significantly, *Defending the Caveman's* creator and performer believes men have a bad rap. Becker points out that women say "men are all assholes" with a kind of feminist cultural authority men don't enjoy (anymore) when they make derogatory remarks about women. Becker, thus, echoes the common sentiment among American men today that men are in the untenable position of being both hated and ignorant. They may want to try, but they are unable to succeed. Feminist psychologist Cheryl Travis comments that this show "offer[s] reassurance about the natural basis for unequal political privilege."[35] But we must also face the fact that men, and women, really enjoy this show. It validates their observations of the behavior patterns and sex battles in their daily lives, and seems to poke fun at men's shortcomings.

Computer programmer Craig Hagstrom writes about the philosophical significance of understanding our evolved tendencies in *The Passionate Ape: Bad Sex, Strong Love, and Human Evolution*, in which he focuses on sex, dating, and mating. His conclusion: men evolved to be, at best, incompetent partners to women. It can be worse, too, according to Hagstrom: "The average man is bigger and stronger than the average woman, and might pose a real threat if angered. He's bristly in the morning, and sex with him usually won't give her orgasms."[36] It's hard to say how many people read Hagstrom's book, but it was reviewed on a popular Internet site and Hagstrom himself has a Web site promoting his book's ideas as well as his speaking tour.[37] And, although he presumes that humans evolved in the water and he is not an academic, Hagstrom's Web site lists recommended readings, which include books by HBE scholars, such as Richard Dawkins, Sarah Blaffer Hrdy, Desmond Morris, Frans De Waal, and E. O. Wilson.[38] My point is not that these scholars would like Hagstrom's book (as certainly their books are far more sagacious), but that Hagstrom offers a version of evolutionary thinking gleaned from his reading of HBE scholarship.

Hagstrom exemplifies the idea that all men are potential rapists, noting,

> Sexual assault is not only the typical act of a bad person but also a bad act of a typical one. Men and women need to know that this barely caged predatory instinct always rides uninvited in the back seat, with only training holding it at bay.[39]

He mourns the missing relationship potential in men—a potential that, he argues, evolution bred out of them: "Intelligence is clearly a disposable asset in humans, and when it caused trouble we shed some. But, like seeing senility, it is tragic to feel what has slipped away."[40] Here is how Hagstrom describes the compromises men and women must make given their divergent evolved desires:

> Men and women meet at a mental village green, at the edge of each sex's normal behavior.... We might all like the opposite sex to live closer to our ideal. Women's self-repression given free reign would ban pornography.... But purely sexual images are only daydreams of men's ancestral sexuality, and their relations with females long-since dead.... Men disdain romances some women read by the hundreds. Average men can't hope to match the powerful, intimate, passionate men in those stories, any more than women can live up to the easy sexuality men like to view.... We might (but I don't propose to) ban these as emotional pornography harmful to men.[41]

In the end, the computer scientist's message is similar to that of the HBE scholars who've commented on human nature and the importance of admitting our animal natures: recognize your biological original sin and exercise free will to move beyond it for greater meaning in life. As Hagstrom puts it,

> We can intentionally improve our situation only by choosing what to accomplish and knowing what to overcome. I don't mean to justify how things work, but to appraise forces we must deal with. We got this far by natural selection, and in the process inherited unruly instincts. To amend our behavior and injure each other less often, we need to see the path and the obstacles.[42]

#1　Fuck it?

#2　Kill it?

Fuck It or Kill It?

One final pop-culture adaptation of HBE ideas is worth mentioning because it is humorous and quite obviously has the good intention of making men better people. In *The Silverback Gorilla Syndrome*, organizational consultant and nature lover Jeff Hood uses the logic of "let's face that we're cavemen" to get men to become more compassionate and peaceful. His introduction explains,

> In the course of emerging from the jungles of our primate ancestors, we have stumbled onto, some would say earned, a thing called awareness. This faculty has spawned a body of knowledge leading to science, industry, technology—and ultimately increased comfort and longer lives. But it has also sparked an illusion of separation from the rest of the animal kingdom. Forging ahead in the quest for control over our destiny and our planet, we act as if the laws of nature do not apply to us. We are blind to the many ways

in which the dominant attitudes and competitive behavior we have inherited threaten to push us dangerously out of balance with our world.

Our saving grace may be to use our awareness instead for tempering the silverback gorilla syndrome that has brought us success at such great cost. This book is an attempt to increase that awareness.[43]

To explain all men's inner gorilla, the author cleverly develops a character called "Big G" who "approaches every social situation with one of two questions: #1 Fuck it? #2 Kill it?"[44] Of course, Hood's aim is to get men to embrace this inner gorilla and use him for good and not evil, to learn not to act on questions 1 or 2 in all circumstances, even though it's inevitable that those questions will be asked. Hood offers the same message that, as I argued in chapter 2, HBE scholars do: gain knowledge of who you really are as an evolved man to overcome your biological original sin and be a nicer guy.

Let me be clear: *The Silverback Gorilla Syndrome* is a delightful little book. It's funny; it has good motivations. Hood recognizes the common problems of contemporary Western masculinity: fierce competition in the workplace, a lack of introspection and authentic relationships, and a reliance on cunning and bluffery to maintain one's self-image or position of power. This form of masculinity is an exhausting, life-threatening charade that costs men their marriages and their health and threatens the entire planet due to the destruction men wreak on the environment and on other people. Hood wants to turn men into responsible, compassionate creatures, insisting that awareness of that inner gorilla—Big G—is the only way out.

In getting to know his inner gorilla, Hood explains that a man will

> discover that he is always "on the make," that he loves to compete and relishes a juicy challenge. These are simply expressions of his passion for life.... . our King of the Jungle needs a job, a quest, a worthy outlet for his passion in life. He needs opportunities to thump his chest every once in a while. Occasionally, he may need to be wild, as well. Above all, he needs to experience joy! This simple, primal emotion is one a gorilla can hang his hat on.[45]

As I discussed in chapter 2, HBE theory is often used in an attempt to save men. The type of reform HBE theory offers may be better than men not changing at all, but the perspective and the change it prompts are limited. Like the Promise Keepers, the Christian organization of men who devote themselves to their wives, but expect to remain heads of their

Gorilla in Pants, from Jeff Hood's *Silverback Gorilla Syndrome*.

households,[46] HBE-style reform offers a soft patriarchy. Men reformed via an evolutionary consciousness are still going to see themselves as superior to women and naturally aggressive. Even the most well-meaning adaptations of HBE theory never question the idea of men's heterosexual, aggressive inner core or evolved psychology. As such, they have a limited ability to move beyond the assumptions that lead so many others to use the same basic theory to rationalize being boorish. But as I will show in chapter 5, this you-can-be-saved-with-awareness-of-your-biological-original-sin approach will be less effective than transforming the cultural consciousness about the way the body, sex, and science are understood.

The Caveman as Embodied Ethos

If the evolutionary stories appeal to many men, and it seems that indeed they do, it's because they ring true. Many men feel like their bodies are aggressive. These guys feel urges, at a physical level, in line with evolutionary theoretical predictions. With a naive understanding of experience, men can see affect as having an authenticity and empirical validity to it. In other words, those men who feel like cavemen do not see their identity as a fiction; it is their bodily reality and it is backed by scientific study.

HBE scholars would certainly argue that the actual evolved psychologies make men feel like cavemen, or at least make those feelings emerge or affect behavior in particular environments. In this section, I argue that this explanation too simplistically separates bodies from discourse.

I will use here the theory of *habitus* advanced by the late sociologist Pierre Bourdieu to suggest that popular manifestations of scientific evolutionary narratives about men's sexuality have a real material effect on many men. Bourdieu's work provides a tool for understanding how power is organized at the level of unconscious embodiment of cultural forces. His theory of practice develops the concepts of *habitus* and *field* to describe a reciprocally constitutive relationship between bodily dispositions and dominant power structures. Bourdieu concerns himself primarily with the ways in which socioeconomic class is incorporated at the level of the body, including class-based ways of speaking, postures, lifestyles, attitudes, and tastes.

Significant for Bourdieu is that people acquire tastes that mark them as members of particular social groups and particular social levels.[47] Membership in a particular social class produces and reproduces a class sensibility, what Bourdieu calls "practical sense."[48] Habitus is "a somatized social relationship, a social law converted into an embodied law."[49] The process of becoming competent in the everyday life of a society or group constitutes habitus. Bourdieu's notion of embodiment can be extended to suggest that habitus, as embodied field, amounts to "the pleasurable and ultimately erotic constitution of [the individual's] social imaginary."[50]

Concerning the circulation of evolutionary narratives, we can see men taking erotic pleasure in the formation of male identity and the performance of accepted norms of heterosexual masculinity using precisely these tools of popular evolutionary science. Put differently, pop-Darwinism is a discourse that finds its way into men's bones and boners. The caveman story can become a man's practical sense of who he is and what he desires. This is so because masculinity is a dimension of embodied and performative practical sensibility—because men carry themselves with a bodily comportment suggestive of their position as the dominant gender, and they invest themselves in particular lifestyle practices, consumption patterns, attire, and bodily comportment. Evolutionary narratives thus enter the so-called habitus, and an aestheticized discourse and image of the caveman circulates through popular culture, becoming part of natural perception, and consequently is reproduced by those embodying it.

In his study of the overwhelmingly white and male workspace of the San Francisco Options Exchange floor, sociologist Richard Widick uses Bourdieu's theory to explain the traders' physical and psychical engagement with their work. Widick holds that "the traders' inhabitation and practical mastery of the trading floor achieves the bio-physical psychosocial state of a natural identity."[51] Hence, the traders describe their manner as a "trading instinct." In a similar way, American men with what we might call a caveman instinct can be said to have acquired a "pre-reflexive practical sense" of themselves as heterosexually driven.[52]

Bourdieu gives the name "symbolic violence" to that process by which we come to accept and embody power relations without ever accepting them in the conscious sense of knowing them and choosing them. We hold beliefs that don't need to be thought—the effects of which can be "durably and deeply embedded in the body in the form of dispositions."[53] From this perspective, the durable dispositions of evolutionary discourse are apparent in our rape culture, for example, when a man sexually assaulting a woman says, "Welcome back to the caveman times." Embodying the ideology of irrepressible heterosexual desire makes such aggression appear to be natural.

The field of power-laden social and cultural differences ensures the formation of differentiated habitus, which will in turn structure social behavior and identification in ways that perpetuate existing inequalities. Political inequalities inhere within a person as habitus, such that they themselves can be judged and found wanting or, alternatively, found fitting, by virtue of reference to the cultural formation it makes manifest.[54] Habitus thus enables a man to feel normal and pass judgment on others with a different habitus, while constraining him to tend to certain forms of established judgment.[55]

Bourdieu's theory allows us to see that both cultural and material forces reveal themselves in the lived reality of social relations.[56] We can see on men's bodies the effects of their struggle with slipping economic privilege and a sense of entitlement to superiority over women. If men live out power struggles in their everyday experiences, then the caveman mystique can be seen as an imagined compensation for men's growing sense of pow-erlessness.[57] To be sure, some men have more social and economic capital than others. Those with less might invest even more in their bodies and appearances.[58]

In a discussion of the significance of naturalizing male power, sociolo-gist R. W. Connell notes,

> The physical sense of maleness is not a simple thing. It involves size and shape, habits of posture and movement, particular physical skills and the lack of others, the image of one's own body, the way it is presented to other people and the ways they respond to it, the way it operates at work and in sexual relations. In no sense is all this a consequence of XY chro-mosomes, or even of the possession on which discussions of masculinity have so lovingly dwelt, the penis. The physical sense of maleness grows through a personal history of social practice, a life-history-in-society.[59]

We see and believe that men's power over women is the order of nature because "power is translated not only into mental body images and fanta-sies, but into muscle tensions, posture, the feel and texture of the body."[60] Scientific discourse constitutes the field for some men in the constructed figure of the caveman, enabling those men to internalize such an identity. The caveman, thus, becomes an imaginative projection that is experienced and lived as real biological truth.

In *Cultural Boundaries of Science,* Thomas Gieryn comments on the cultural authority of science, suggesting that "if 'science' says so, we are more often than not inclined to believe it or act on it—and to prefer it to claims lacking this epistemic seal of approval."[61] To his observation I would add that we are also more likely to *live* it. Ideas that count as sci-entific, regardless of their truth value, become lived ideologies. It's how modern American men have become cavemen and how the caveman ethos enjoys reproductive success.

Cultural anthropologist Paul Rabinow gives the name *biosociality* to the formation of new group and individual identities and practices that emerge from the scientific study of human life.[62] Rabinow offers the example of groups for those afflicted with neurofibromatosis, whose mem-bers gather to discuss their experiences, educate their children, lobby for their disease, and "understand" their fate. And in the future, he points out, "It is not hard to imagine groups formed around the chromosome 17, locus 16,256, site 654,376 allele variant with a guanine substitution."[63]

Rabinow's concept of biosociality is instructive here, for the discourse of the caveman offers this form of biosociality. The caveman constitutes an identity based on new scientific "facts" about one's biology.

Of course, evolutionary psychologists would have us think that men's desires are, in some final instance, biological properties of an internal psyche or sexual psychology. I am suggesting, in line with Bourdieu, that men's desires are always performed in relation to the dominant discourses in circulation within their cultural life worlds, either for or against the representations that permeate those life worlds. We can see that a significant number of men are putting the pop-Darwinist rhetoric to good use in social interactions. The scientific discourse of the caveman (however unscientific we might regard it by the time it gets to everyday guys reading magazines and watching TV) is corporealized, quite literally incorporated into living identities, deeply shaping these men's experiences of being men.

In telling men a story about who they are, naturally, pop-Darwinism has the normalizing, disciplinary effect of forging a common, biological identity among men. Embodying ideology allows men to feel morally exonerated while they reproduce that very ideology. The discourse of male biological unity suppresses many significant differences among men, and, of course, many ways in which men would otherwise identify with women's tastes and behaviors.

In the next chapter I suggest that nothing about the theory of evolution itself actually demands that we retain a view of predatory male heterosexuality. The popularity of evolutionary explanations for men's behavior rests in part on the cultural purchase science enjoys. But what if we were less sure of what science can tell us about our evolutionary past? What if the evolutionary record isn't as straight at it seems? The next chapter first explores the ways in which our existing gender politics inform evolutionary theorizing and then disrupts the certainty of that scientific knowledge. I show that both the scientific objectivity of HBE must be questioned in addition to the hypotheses and interpretations typically pursued by HBE theorists.

4

HOMO SEXUAL

PERVERTING EVOLUTIONARY
STORIES OF MALE SEXUALITY

How to Pervert Evolutionary Theory

Anyone questioning the natural and, therefore, privileged status of heterosexuality today is likely to meet up with an evolutionary narrative: "After all, how could the human species have survived without heterosexuality?" Chapter 2 showed that science, and Darwinism in particular, replaced Christianity as an authoritative account of human nature used to settle political disputes. Furthermore, chapter 3 argued that popular cultural knowledge about heterosexual masculinity is increasingly informed by evolutionary accounts of human nature that are generated formally by scientists and then passed along in the popular press. The caveman narrative, when presented as an authoritative science of who men are, can make men *feel* like cavemen—that is, primally and rampantly heterosexual.

Being wild and untamed means, for many in this culture, being heterosexual. After all, to be civil is to be urbane, gracious, well-mannered, well-groomed—the qualities associated culturally with being effete. And if a man is refined, well-mannered, conversational, and wears a fashionable shirt with socks to match it, he's routinely suspected of being gay. Declaring an inability to be bred socially and claiming an innate heterosexuality go together like beer and belching.

The idea of, and compulsion to live out, "manhood" as a natural category that is innately heterosexual has enabled and rationalized a whole host of social ills—notably, queer-bashing and rape.[1] And while pop-Darwinism has fueled the story of innate male heterosexuality, this chapter will show that the evolutionary record is not as straight as many think. There is more than one meaning to assign to various species' sexual behaviors and more than one way to imagine *Homo sapiens*' evolutionary history. Such a "queer reading" of evolution exposes current evolutionary stories as heterocentrist and thus might interrupt a principal method of privileging heterosexuality and rationalizing those social ills. This queer reading of evolution suggests that human behavior and evolution (HBE) ideas appeal in part because they allow men to claim their inner rudeness—their inability to be civil— through a related claim that they are innately heterosexual.

Current evolutionary narratives provide a framework for making heterosexual behaviors seem more legitimate (more "natural") than others. Paradoxically, the prevailing commitment to heterosexuality serves as the framework for the interpretation of our evolutionary history. Evolutionary theories specify "natural" aspects of contemporary human sexuality—"perversions" of which can be theorized, condemned, or mocked by those who consider themselves properly and primally heterosexual. Since sex—in the essentialist discourse of modernism—has been thought of as a natural essence geared toward reproduction, sexual acts that do not lead to or imitate reproduction (e.g., masturbation, cunnilingus, anal intercourse, sadomasochistic sex) have been considered "unnatural," and, by virtue of close association of the natural with the morally acceptable, immoral.

Although falsely impartial, absolutist frameworks are not necessary for determining the legitimacy of various behaviors, we all need contingent frameworks to argue for or against any practice.[2] That we need such frameworks is not the problem. The problem is that science has not been an explicitly political discourse, but instead enjoys a discursive position as absolute authority, as though "objective" knowledge exists and scientific knowledge is it. For example, such presumably neutral knowledge is often invoked to settle political disputes authoritatively, like whether or not homosexuality is a crime or a psychological disorder. Evolutionary narratives persistently appear in popular American cultural texts and have tremendous appeal in a Judeo–Christian foundationalist culture that tends to justify heterosexual privilege by appealing to falsely impartial scientific versions of nature. Evolutionary justifications for the dominant status of heterosexuality have extended, and nearly replaced, Judeo–Christian ones.[3]

Evolutionary science is far from impartial, however; at present, an ideology of heterosexism colors it. Heterosexism is then perpetuated, in a vicious circle, through its grounding in scientific stories whose authority depends upon a refusal to acknowledge their implication in ideology and politics. Scientists do not think that the evolutionary past that they construct is imaginary. They think they have evidence that supports their construction of our past. This evidence, however, is interpreted through an unacknowledged heterocentrist framework.

My assumption is not that evolutionary theories are heterosexist and bad *because they (mis)interpret nature* (what some feminists might claim); nor that evolutionary theories make what is *really* cultural out to be natural (what some social constructionists might claim); nor that feminists and queers just don't like to admit what evolutionary theories innocently reveal (as some evolutionary theorists might claim). All of these statements assume that science is necessarily at odds with constructionism, or that evolutionary theory is necessarily at odds with feminist and queer theories. It is my aim here to undermine the evolutionary naturalization of heterosexuality, but not by arguing that evolutionary theory itself is the enemy. Such an approach would conflate the heterocentrist background assumptions in evolutionary narratives with the logic of evolution itself and ignore the highly consequential character of scientific stories. Nor do I pervert evolutionary narratives of heterosexual masculinity by advancing some indisputable "truth" of humanity's queer evolutionary history, an approach that would affirm rather than undermine the naturalization of identities and the authority of science to settle political disputes.

I want to expose the values behind heterocentrist scientific accounts— not to replace them with an impossibly value-neutral account, but, rather, with an equally sensible evolutionary theory laden with values accountable to queers. As social theorist Steven Seidman puts it, science is "a powerful practical-moral force."[4] I engage evolutionary stories not to offer the final truth of our evolutionary history, to biologize even more identities, to stabilize identity itself, or to undermine heterosexism through my own infeasibly detached account of nature. Rather, I offer an alternative story that could function as a different, equally plausible, consequential evolutionary myth. This myth, unlike the more popular heterocentrist one whose consequence is to naturalize heterosexual manhood, might make heterosexuality seem less instinctual. This, in turn, might pave the way for greater tolerance for those who do not identify as heterosexual, of the flexibility of identities, and more generally of the instability of knowledge about those identities.

My intervention proceeds from two related axioms. First, from feminist critiques of science,[5] the generation of scientific knowledge is always a value-laden cultural practice, often containing irreflexive (hetero)sexist assumptions that naturalize gender and sexuality. Second, from queer theory,[6] cultural texts—in this case scientific texts—can be read as queer. These queer meanings are no more or less value-laden than the straight meanings already associated with them. "Queering" evolutionary theory involves offering a new scientific story in a way that exposes the political character of all knowledge claims. Insisting upon the legitimacy of another (queer) narrative calls into question not only the hegemonic narrative, but the stable, "objective" status of identities and scientific representations more generally.

For this reason, I suggest that linking homosexuality to biology through scientific research is the wrong approach. Although the idea of a "gay gene" or a "gay brain" might appeal to many who have been pressured to "unlearn" their "deviant" sexuality, and to many who have justified discriminatory practices on the grounds that homosexuality is "unnatural," such an approach leaves in place, and even cements, the status of heterosexuality as natural and normative and, further, the status of scientific stories as value-neutral accounts of human nature. I want to offer a strategy that takes heterosexuality out of its privileged position as *the* natural adaptation grounded in human evolutionary history.

I employ evolutionary theory with a homophilic rather than homophobic set of background assumptions in order to show that the theory of evolution could undermine as easily as it enables the privileged status of heterosexual relationships and sex acts. By exposing the heterocentrist assumptions in theoretical and popular interpretations of evolution, I present evidence of the inescapably political character of scientific stories,[7] and thus of the ease with which any political claim can be justified by "nature" and, further, of the ensuing impossibility of securing any political rights in "nature."

Biological theories of the gay brain or gay gene do not feasibly secure gay rights precisely because of the inevitably political character of all scientific accounts of nature, and because those theories fail to dislodge heterosexuality from its position as biologically normative and fail to challenge the position of scientific stories of nature as value-free. Exposing the political character of falsely naturalized accounts of heterosexual male desire is a more promising strategy for undermining heterocentrist knowledge.

Evolution and Evolutionary Theory Are Already Perverted

Chapter 3 provided evidence of the popularity of caveman stories, conveying both the consequential character of evolutionary stories about male sexuality and the political urgency of alternative accounts. I won't repeat those examples here, but I will provide a few more examples of the ways that evolutionary theories, both professional and popular, normalize heterosexuality—even when considering unusual sexual forms. I want to consider the ways in which the increasingly popular evolutionary discourse on the sexual practices of insects, birds, and mammals enables the construction of naturalized heterosexual masculine identities. Without wishing to impute conspiracy or stupidity, I suggest that heterocentrist background assumptions (including an unexamined commitment to heterosexuality as a natural and/or privileged institution and identity) in evolutionary theoretical interpretation reinscribe evolutionary stories within a heterosexist logic.

One year after prominent sociobiologist David Barash published his now well-known 1977 article in *Science* on the sociobiology of rape in mallard ducks, he published a more general evolutionary adaptationist view of the mating practices of various birds in *Psychology Today*, mentioning the significance of sociobiology for the study of human beings.[8] Scott Morris, a writer for *Playboy*, eventually saw this and composed an article, "Darwin and the Double Standard" with this subtitle: "It has been said that a man will try to make it with anything that moves—and a woman won't. Now the startling new science of sociobiology tells us why."[9] While providing a vocabulary of motive for adulterous heterosexual male readers, this article's parodic style so thoroughly enmeshes human values with accounts of what's going on in nature that the possibility of using evolution as an unproblematic foundation to justify or condemn a sexual practice becomes difficult. There are so many different mating habits—such as the female praying mantis's habit of beheading and eating the male while he mounts her, or that of the California seagull, which is characterized by female pair bonds who mount one another and hatch eggs together, using the male gull only for fertilization—that the story could justify any reader's "perversion."

Playboy's lampoonish elucidation of evolved mating habits illustrates what people inevitably do with scientific renderings of nature—alloy them with their values from and visions of social life. For instance, Morris explains the California seagull this way:

Jonathan Livingston Lesbian

California lady gulls are A.C./D.C. When there aren't enough males to go around, females pair up with each other. One even becomes a bull dyke: She mounts the other, defends the nest and does courtship feeding just like a male normally would. (No, she doesn't get a short haircut!) These 'odd couples' lay eggs and sometimes they even hatch! Virgin births? Hardly. It seems that there are lecherous males about who, though happily married, are not averse to a bit on the side. And, we're happy to report, our gay females are easily beguiled into accepting even a one-night stand. That way, they get to have some offspring and each other, too.[10]

And, Morris gives this description of wild turkeys:

Cruising

Male wild turkeys travel in pairs. They both cooperate in dancing about to impress the lady turkeys, but when it's actually time to screw, one of the males consistently lets the other do it all. What's going on here? The association between males clearly benefits the one who gets to do all the mating, but what's in it for the subordinate Alphonse? Is he *really* a turkey? In fact, he is often Gaston's *brother*, so, though not a father, he is at least guaranteed being an uncle to milady's chicks.[11]

Although quite heterosexist, these anecdotes frolic in the value-laden character of nature stories. Morris's style winds up using scientific theories less than satirizing them.

A parallel queer (sub)version of evolutionary theory is possible (something I attempt later in this chapter), but mating stories usually become reinscribed in a heterocentrist language, presupposing and reinforcing a paradigmatically heterosexual position. The cover story of a 1992 issue of *Time*—"Why Are Men and Women Different?"—is illustrative. The article includes a section called "How Other Species Do It" and explains that "nature follows more than one script."[12] Just after mentioning that some species do not even have two sexes, author Christine Gorman explains one such species (cichlids) this way:

These fish come in three sexes: brightly hued macho males, paler females, and male wimps that look and act like females. There are only a few sexually active males in a school. But the minute a piscine Lothario dies, an ambitious wimp rises to the occasion. His brain unleashes sex hormones that bring color to his scales and make him feisty, but he can revert to pallid impotence if challenged by a more macho fish.[13]

Gorman's description fails to escape a male/female conceptual framework: the third sex can only be called "male wimps that look and act like females." This language also takes male cichlids who are attracted to or actively seeking breeding opportunities with females to be the norm, and the more flexible fish to be odd. This story of the cichlid preserves precisely what another description of the cichlid could call into question: our criteria for gender assignment. This account, like many of those in the popular men's magazines and the less widely read scientific journals, is brimming with the values and discursive categories of a heterosexist patriarchal culture.

A privileged, naturalized heterosexuality—with its concurrent masculine and feminine dispositions making up an auspicious nuclear family unit—is an implicit part of the framework for evolutionary interpretation and its reiterations in the popular press. Commonly held assumptions about gender and sexuality make up a strong conceptual filter through which scientific evidence is understood.[14] This filter, especially when ignored, prevents data that might be taken as evidence that contradicts the privileged status of heterosexuality from being seen as such. For example, Gorman explains men's better scores on tests that require three-dimensional thought by emphasizing "ancient evolutionary pressures related to hunting, which requires orienting oneself while pursuing prey."[15] Women's better scores on tests that require remembering locations of objects are explained by "evolutionary pressure on generations of women who foraged for their food. Foragers must recall complex patterns formed of apparently unconnected items."[16] "Orienting oneself" and "recalling complex patterns" are vague enough so that if the gendered patterns in test scores were reversed it could be assumed that men needed to "recall complex patterns" for hunting and women needed to "orient themselves" while foraging. The point is that data are not used to question the presumed man-the-hunter, woman-the-gatherer scenario. As philosopher of science Helen Longino has pointed out, the values in scientific inquiry influence the hypotheses for which the data are taken as evidence.[17] Gorman's evolutionary account of current Western gender differences in test scores supports the hetero-centrist model because it already assumes it.

Heterosexual Masculinity as the Origin of the
Origins of Heterosexual Masculinity

Many evolutionary accounts, without even acknowledging the existence of gays and lesbians, construct accounts about sexuality that could challenge some aspects of the presumed naturalness of heterosexuality, but simply ignore any possible challenge and instead fit the theory into an *a priori* model of natural heterosexuality. For example, Desmond Morris makes the claim that breasts look like buttocks.[18] His argument is that men are attracted to women's shapes, including their hindquarters, because men have evolved to spot signals of fertility—from the front or the back. He seems to be forgetting that both men and women have buttocks. He also forgets that many women's breasts don't look at all like buttocks; they are either not round and bulbous or they are too small, whatever their shape, to resemble buttocks.

Jared Diamond's 1997 HBE book *Why is Sex Fun?* considers the fact that the human male penis is far larger than that of any of our primate relatives.[19] Diamond argues that the size of the penis in the human male was limited by the capacity of the human female vagina:

> Starting from a 1½-inch ancestral ape penis similar to the penis of a modern gorilla or orangutan, the human penis increased in length by a runaway process, conveying an advantage to its owner as an increasingly conspicuous signal of virility, until its length became limited by counterselection as difficulties fitting into a woman's vagina became imminent.[20]

Diamond also argues that penis size is a trade-off with brain size; therefore, the human male penis announces, according to Diamond, "I'm already so smart and superior that I don't need to devote more ounces of protoplasm to my brain, but I can instead afford the handicap of packing the ounces uselessly into my penis."[21] But, he concedes,

> What remains debatable is the intended audience at which the penis's proclamation of virility is directed. ... the ones really fascinated by the penis and its dimensions are men. In the showers in men's locker rooms, men routinely size up each other's endowment.[22]

In the end, Diamond concludes that if the large human male penis was designed, in the evolutionary sense, to impress men, such an impression was not sexual, but a confirmation of dominance over male rivals who might be competing for sexual access to women.[23] Now, a male peacock's colorful plumage impresses peahens. A male deer with a rack of antlers uses that rack to fight off other males entering his mating turf. But, the sight of a 5-inch penis by one carrying a 4-inch one? Exactly how this would establish dominance Diamond never discusses.

Diamond takes for granted that women's vaginal length limited the size of men's penises. He offers no acknowledgment that men do other sexual things with their penises. Diamond's is a book about sex and why it's fun, but nowhere in this book does he discuss the fun of homosexual sex. He simply presumes that all sex—at least all sex to which evolutionary theory is worth applying—is heterosexual sex. While he admits that there are unresolved questions about the evolution of penis size, his discussion of the selective forces that might have driven the development of the large human penis is completely heterocentrist.

Robin Baker's *Sperm Wars* stands out as a significant exception among HBE books intended for a wide audience.[24] Baker includes a chapter titled "One Way or Another" to discuss the ways in which bisexuality is a reproductive strategy: "Far from being a pathway to a lower level of reproductive success, homosexual inclination is very much a successful reproductive alternative to heterosexuality."[25] Though unusual for discussing bisexuality at some length, Baker's language gives the false impression that bisexuals are actually trying to enhance their reproductive success, perhaps allowing a reader to imagine that bisexuality is a "mating strategy"—and ultimately heterosexual and breeding oriented.[26]

Other HBE scholars focus on characteristics of interest to Western heterosexual men, such as rape and sexual harassment of women, explaining heterosexual men's behavior toward women as evolved aspects of male sexual psychology. In other words, evolutionary theorists take heterosexual male behaviors and theorize the circumstances in the environment of evolutionary adaptedness (the hunting and gathering part of our human history; hereafter, EEA) for which they, even if in less extreme form, would have been beneficial.

Evolutionary psychologists Michael Studd and Urs Gattiker argue that the prevalence of sexual harassment in organizations is evidence for the existence of evolved psychological mechanisms:

[T]he workplace environment especially appears to push male behavior toward [the] threshold [for coercive sexual behavior] by increasing the opportunity and stimuli for sexual advances, and by minimizing the opportunity for recipients of unwanted sexual advances to avoid such attention.[27]

They claim that their study will "further strengthen the validity and extend the domain of the science of evolutionary psychology."[28] Strengthening the validity of the idea that men's behavior toward women can be accounted for biologically is their goal; the problem of sexual harassment seems secondary—simply the vehicle used in a search for man's true nature and the strength of HBE theory. Their justification of their endeavor supposes that only a (presumably) apolitical truth about man's nature could actually provide a solution to such social problems anyway.

Studd and Gattiker remind readers that they do not mean to imply that women should begin to forgive sexual harassers:

It is simply our hope that the more we understand about the evolution of human psychology, the closer we will be to developing appropriate and effective solutions for such unfortunate and deplorable side effects of human nature and behavior as sexual harassment.[29]

Their solution involves changing

the structure of the organizational environment which would reduce the stimulus and opportunity for evolved male sexual psychology to motivate the initiation of sexual advances, and allow women more freedom to change jobs or change their working environment, as they feel is necessary.[30]

Allowing harassers more "freedom" to get fired is not mentioned as a solution, nor is equal pay, although earlier the authors state that women's economic position relative to men's makes this male strategy surface (the way lots of gardening makes calluses come out). They conclude by underscoring the importance of evolutionary psychology for handling the problem of sexual harassment: "With the knowledge provided by an understanding of the evolutionary psychology of human behavior, we have the opportunity to make a positive contribution toward the management of sexual harassment… ."[31] (No doubt this would *manage* sexual harassment rather than end it.) As stated in chapter 2, such righteous proclamations position evolutionary science as a beacon of hope with regard to men's bad behaviors.

Grounding men's harassing behavior in evolutionary psychology assumes that sexual harassment is rooted in an urge to initiate copulation, when a significant amount of harassment goes on without an interest in copulation on the part of the harasser and without the result of copulation (e.g., when a man is constantly making sexist jokes, hanging up photos of naked women, touching women, looking down a woman's blouse, etc.).[32] Given their assumption that sexual harassment is some sort of courtship behavior, its extremely low success rate provides ample reason to wonder how any harassing males could have had enough successful breeding opportunities to pass this trait on.[33]

The existence of sexual harassment could be, but never is, taken as evidence that heterosexuality is not evolved. But so strong is the heterocentrist bias that Studd and Gattiker instead theorize that there was probably no evolutionary pressure against male "mistakes" of harassment—that is, the initiation of sexual contact when a woman is not interested. They explain how privileged ignorance is an evolved psychological mechanism in men:

> [I]f proceptivity (i.e. showing signs of sexual interest when such interest exists) is an evolved part of female sexual psychology, one would expect males to have co-evolved psychological mechanisms sensitive to this type of female behavior and which motivate the initiation of sexual overtures in response. Males in past environments who lacked this psychological response would have been selected against by missing limited opportunities to pursue matings with interested females... Missing a real opportunity for sexual access would be ultimately more costly than occasionally misreading signals of female availability. Thus, males may have evolved psychological mechanisms which cause them to "deliberately," but unconsciously, *misinterpret* female signals of friendliness and sociality as sexual in nature.[34]

This view posits an imperceptiveness on the part of men. But a *Muscle and Fitness* magazine discussion of evolved male tendencies to ogle at women supposes a high degree of male perceptiveness with respect to what women look like. Evolutionary theorists reason that men's great number of sperm renders men perpetually in heat, if you will. As we read in the *Muscle and Fitness* article,

> A man's genetic stock went up every time he got a woman pregnant. As long as he could do so with low risk and little cost of time or energy,

natural selection favored "his tendency to be aroused sexually by the sight of women."[35]

Further, men are always evaluating what women look like, and are attracted to specific types of female appearances—namely, those that indicate fertility, such as "smooth skin, long hair and fingernails and white teeth."[36]

As I mentioned in chapter 3, HBE scholar David Buss argues that men who were not picky about women's looks are not our ancestors.[37] Buss' view simply assumes that men in the EEA had particular preferences for mates and then mated with only those types of people. In other words, it assumes that men who mated with infertile people never mated with fertile people. In contrast, the theory of sexual harassment based on the assumption that men have evolved to sometimes read the non-sexual signals of women as sexual signals works by presuming that the men with less keen sensitivities toward women would have had the evolutionary edge. In other words, the sex harassment theory reasons that it must have been better for men just to go for it rather than be cautious about whom they are mating with, while the ogling theory presumes that it must have been better to be cautious or choosy about appearances than to go for sex with anyone.

Male ogling can be explained evolutionarily only if we assume first that men can, or could ever, spot fertility accurately, and second that men who had such a keen ability to make such distinctions among women actually had more offspring that lived to reproductive age. But if men's great number of sperm make their ejaculations so nugatory, evolution could have conceivably favored men who find all women physically appealing or who mate without regard to appearance or fertility. There would have been no cost for male "mistakes" of ejaculating into infertile bodies,[38] and thus no selective pressure against men who did not distinguish between fertile and infertile people. Men who mated licentiously may have wound up with more of their genes in the population. The men who mated with both fertile and infertile people would have reproduced this "tendency." Men may not have mated exclusively with fertile females, or even exclusively with females. Indeed, ancestral men may have made no distinction between fertile and infertile females as objects of sexual desire; they may have made no distinction between males and females as objects of sexual desire.

The behavior of today's average Western heterosexual man cannot provide uncomplicated evidence of a specific evolved sexual psychology or of what the EEA was like, any more than people's sugar cravings (whether or not these cravings are considered biological) provide evidence that there were candy bars in the EEA[39] (the sort of mistake evolutionary theorists make when talking about male sexuality, but not when talking about eating sweets).[40] If people in the EEA were not particularly focused on sex and matings, or if such occasions were not readily available to them, then there would not have been any selective pressure limiting sexual capacity. After all, it's not as if ancestral men lived in cities with strip joints. Rather, they likely lived in relative visual isolation from the women to whom they were not related. Thus, men's current sexual capacities do not imply that most men in the EEA sought the sexual attention of women specifically or very often, or that doing so would have made one more reproductively competitive. Assuming this from any of today's heterosexual male behaviors and/or expressed desires is like assuming that there must have been lots of candy in the EEA, that those who ate lots of sweets were more reproductively successful, and that the reason we eat sweets today is because our ancestors ate a lot of sweets, which must have been good for them.

Consider the men to whom the *Muscle and Fitness* article may have been speaking. Its suggestion that men are wired to look lustfully, combined with the statement on the magazine cover that purports to explain "Why Women Lust After Muscular Men," may offer a veiled evolutionary justification for gay male readers who lust after muscular men. Evolutionary theorists could admit that there are plenty of men who are not particularly interested in women sexually and/or who do not express sexual interest as ogling and harassing.

I am not suggesting that evolutionary theories of male sexual psychology are troubling because they are "just so" stories. Evolutionary theorists explain that, unlike "just so" stories, the stories they produce are responses to hypotheses generated by evolutionary theory. But deplorable behaviors common among Western heterosexual men, like sexual harassment and rape, could be taken as evidence for an entirely different set of hypotheses about the sorts of male and female sexual psychologies for which there was selective pressure in the EEA. Evolutionary theory doesn't prevent these scholars from considering alternative hypotheses for which to provide evolutionary evidence; heterocentrism does.

Homosexuality as Heterosexuality ... as Homosexuality

Another way evolutionary theorists continue to privilege heterosexuality is by explaining homosexual behaviors in terms of their breeding potential or "adaptive value." For instance, David Barash tells *Psychology Today* readers how rape, "even homosexual rape," is rather common in animals "when fitness demands it."[41] The anthocorid bug "rapist" thus "forces" his sperm into the storage organ of his male "victim," sometimes while the "victim" copulates with a female, so that the "victim" transfers the "aggressor bug's" sperm, rather than his own, the next time he copulates with a female (who presumably desires such copulations). Barash provides no evidence that such copulations are forced, which suggests that he is guided by the heterocentrist assumption that a *manly* bug would not allow another male bug to do this to him.[42] Further, Barash presents the male bug "rapist" as if he only copulates with other males in order to gain indirect access to female bugs.[43]

But when the language that attributes intention to the evolutionary process or to individual bugs is suspended, we see that natural selection operated in a way that favored the selection of male bugs who go for sex with other male bugs or sex in groups. Thus, male bugs don't intend to inseminate females (or to "rape" males); the behaviors in question just *feel good*. Darwinists have always said that those behaviors in the EEA that helped an individual survive and reproduce and that were also pleasurable ensured their enactment. The evolutionary story of anthocorid bugs could make homosexuality and other so-called perversions seem more "natural," (and, therefore, more moral, in the modernist, foundationalist logic). Instead, however, homosexual acts become reinscribed in a heterosexual logic, such that anything homosexual must really be for heterosexual/ reproductive purposes.

Yet, a scientist might argue, this is simply (and innocently) adaptationist logic. If a trait leads to the relatively successful reproduction of an individual, then that trait will eventually be selected. Everything must ultimately be explained heterosexually, if you will, since this is the way the beings in question reproduce and traits are selected. However, evolution does not work like an omnipotent designer. Evolution is a bunch of "odd arrangements and funny solutions."[44] Evolutionary theorists' common use of metaphorical shorthand that imputes conscious action or heterosexual intent to genes, natural selection, or individual bugs engaged in "perverted" behavior reinforces the heterosexism of the accounts. A logic of reproductive intent enables the privileging of heterosexuality, and the social impact of such scientific stories serves to make homosexuality "natural" only if it will ultimately be properly heterosexual/mating oriented. However, humans are left behaving in ways that passed on our genes in the EEA, but now just feel good, and may or may not contribute to reproductive success. In other words, ejaculations—heterosexual or homosexual, alone or in groups—just feel good.

Even evolutionary explanations of human homosexuality wind up naturalizing heterosexuality by holding up homosexuality as a challenge for evolutionary theorists to explain—as if the legitimacy of evolutionary theory itself depends upon an evolved heterosexual human nature. A common HBE account of human homosexuality assumes that people who "become" homosexual are from large families and, thus, can "afford," in terms of their inclusive fitness, to live a life without breeding (since they have so many siblings who will be passing on some of their genes).[45] However, this is an explanation of leading an exclusively gay lifestyle rather than an explanation of homosexual attraction or having homosexual experiences. Furthermore, this suggests that homosexuality is a choice made once one's siblings are counted, while evolutionary psychology does not assume that decisions are made with reproductive success in mind. Evolutionary theory can only argue that current decisions are made based on preferences that would have contributed to one's reproductive success back in the EEA. Besides, the argument rests on the assumption that those with a heterosexual identity reproduce and that gay men and lesbians do not. (Perhaps even more gay men and lesbians would have children if heterosexist custody and other laws did not discourage them from doing so.)[46] Finally, such evolutionary explanations of homosexuality marginalize it—and, in so doing, naturalize heterosexuality—by simply assuming that the adaptive value of heterosexuality needs no elucidation.

Evolutionary psychologists Donald Symons and David Buss both discuss gay men, but only to prove the evolutionary roots of heterosexual male attraction. They argue that the allegedly gay male emphasis on youth, physical attractiveness, variation in sexual partners without emotional or financial investment, and genitally and orgasmically focused sex provides evidence for the hypothesis that a male sexual psychological nature exists and is being played out today. Because they reason that gay men do not have to compromise with women's very different sexual psychological nature (as straight men do), Symons and Buss investigate gay male sexuality in order to test their evolutionary theory that ancestral men who were attracted to reproductively healthy, fertile-looking women—and copulated with as many of these as possible, whenever possible, with a minimum of resource investment—would have had greater reproductive success. In other words, as Buss puts it, gay men serve as "an acid test for the evolutionary basis of sex differences in the desires for a mate."[47] However, so strong is the underlying heterocentrist bias that both Symons and Buss seem to miss the obvious irony in studying gay men to provide evidence for the natural basis of heterosexual men's desires.

Assuming that the premises of the argument are correct—that the depiction of tastes properly represents gay men and that such tendencies do have a biological base—the existence of homosexual men shows that evolution may have selected for men who like uncommitted sexual relationships with a variety of good-looking young people, which supports a bisexual or gender-irrelevant hypothesis. Symons and Buss study gay male sexuality, but assume that ancestral men sought youth and beauty in women, rather than in men or without regard to gender. The unconscious commitment to the privileged, natural status of heterosexuality precludes taking homosexuality as evidence for a hypothesis that ancestral males were bisexual.

For these theorists, what could be evidence *against* the naturalness of heterosexuality winds up as more evidence *for* it. Symons merely remarks that the existence of gay men "attests to the importance of *social experience* in determining the objects that humans sexually desire... ."[48] Symons does not argue that "social experience" is necessary for men to be visually stimulated by and want to copulate with a variety of young, beautiful *women*, now or in the EEA. Buss simply dismisses the issue by noting that "[t]he origins of homosexuality remain a mystery."[49] For a scholar who makes his living by explaining the evolutionary basis of current sexual desires, this statement cannot be read simply as scholarly humility; it is a curious omission.

These theoretical attempts take place in a cultural system in which homosexuality is silenced, denied, and wished not to exist.[50] Homosexuality winds up seen either as a problem to be explained in evolutionary theory or as some kinky variation that occurs only when certain environmental conditions do not allow for the heterosexual default mode.[51] The continued implication of animals as strategists, despite the fact that Darwinian psychology asserts a view of adaptation that does not imply that contemporary human action is "rational" in the evolutionary sense, reinforces the heterocentrist assumption. Although the commitment to heterosexuality means that bisexuality is not taken as a hypothesis for which to provide evidence, evolutionary theory could legitimate a variety of sexual practices and bisexuality could be considered an adaptation.

Setting the Evolutionary Record Queer

I have suggested that heterosexual attraction in human beings, and its adaptive value, go unquestioned by evolutionary theorists and their enthusiasts. Consider, though, how easy it is to make a sound evolutionary argument that human bisexuality is evolved.[52] It is not as though human beings needed to mate exclusively with members of the opposite sex in order to survive and reproduce their own genes. For example, evolutionary theorists could take the absence of vaginal orgasm in women as evidence for the existence of an evolved distaste for men or for penile–vaginal intercourse.[53] Women's capacity for multiple clitoral orgasms could indicate that our foremothers may have sought nonpenetrative sexual encounters with men and/or women. Since it was to women's evolutionary advantage not to be pregnant all the time, this set of desires could have been selected for. (Or, it could simply mean that no selective pressure existed to cap off female sexual capacity.)

Edward O. Wilson notes that the primary function of sexual pleasure in human beings is not insemination, but bonding. "All that we can surmise of humankind's genetic history argues for a more liberal sexual morality, in which sexual practices are to be regarded first as bonding devices and only second as means for procreation," he writes.[54] Wilson, however, assumes that men and women bond through sexual relations, whereas men bond with men only because women's year-round "sexual receptivity" makes for less competitive relations between men (due to reduced competition for sexual access to women).[55] But why not imagine the evolutionary benefits of male–male sexual bonds, and postulate the rich sex life that our forefathers might have had with one another— perhaps while away on those hunts? Why not explain the fact that men's buttocks often look more like fertile breasts than women's buttocks do? Why not see a human male's curiously large penis as evidence that men evolved to respond sexually to men as well as women?

It is commonly assumed that the men who had a preference for mating with women rather than men (*assuming* that this is something that could have a genetic component and that such a genetic variation existed among men in the EEA) would have wound up with more offspring, thereby reproducing a trait of male sexual attraction to females. But men have so many expendable sperm that those who were not partial to either sex may have had less competitive relations with other men, and as a result more "breeding opportunities" with females. Wilson assumes that if same-gender sexual bonding occurred it must have been in a small number of people, reasoning that as long as the relatives of a homosexual—who share many of the same genes—were reproductively successful, then the homosexual trait would have been passed on.[56] While more appealing than theories that ignore homosexuality altogether, this narrative is what queer theorist and literature scholar Eve Kosofsky Sedgwick might call a *minoritizing account* of homosexuality.[57] The status of heterosexuality as innate and naturally statistically normative, as a biological-majority orientation, still goes unquestioned.

In line with Sedgwick, illustrator Roz Chast questioned the unquestioned status of heterosexuality as natural with a *New Yorker* magazine cartoon titled "Scientists Discover the Gene for Heterosexuality in Men."[58] The cartoon critiques both scientists' disinterest in searching for a *heterosexual* gene and the common assumption that the many behaviors we associate with sexuality are instinctive. The cartoon presents eight scenarios, each featuring a stereotypical straight white guy, linking the "heterosexual gene" to specific behaviors including: "inability to dance, except for the Texas Two-Step;" "stoic indifference to Judy Garland;" "desire to eat steak and eggs for breakfast;" and "fear of asking directions." Clearly, the cartoon is also clever for turning stereotypically straight—instead of gay—male behaviors into oddities that require scientific explanation.

Rather than keep heterosexuality in its privileged position as a biological-majority orientation, I suggest an account of sexuality that universalizes sexual "deviation:" our ancestors' matings could have been random with regard to genitals. If so, pregnancies would have occurred, babies would have been born, and individuals would have passed on their bisexual tendencies. Heterosexuality would not have been the dominant orientation, with homosexuality a deviant variation practiced by a minority (statistical or otherwise). Gender categories for sexual practices may not have been as distinct as they are today. We simply do not know. The maintenance of a social system in which people must identify with one of two distinct sexes is bound up with the system of compulsory heterosexuality.[59]

Why don't evolutionary theorists argue that ancestral males must have sought opportunities to copulate with either gender? It would not be unreasonable to argue that our heterosexist society (arguably an evolutionarily novel environment) inhibits the options for sexual expression. Within the terms of evolutionary theory itself, bisexuality could be seen as an adaptation, and a society of compulsory hetero-sexuality as, well, *perverted*.

Do Gay Brains Make Better Politics?

Does this new account of human evolution mean then that 10 percent of the human population is naturally homosexual? This claim would not make sense evolutionarily: such a homosexual "trait" would never have reproduced itself, nor do we have evidence that any—let alone 90 percent of—ancestral males were exclusively heterosexual. Nor would this claim make sense sociologically: the categories *homosexual* and *heterosexual*, and their concomitant personal identities, are recent historical constructions.[60] Thus, studies that attempt to legitimate homosexuality by grounding it in biology wind up naturalizing both socially constructed identities and specific boundaries for identification, neither of which may have existed in the human EEA at all. Neurologist Simon LeVay's research—touted in the media as the "gay brain" study—is worth examining because it represents a hopeful attempt to link homosexual desire to biology.[61]

LeVay has suggested that the hypothalamus, a small area over the brain stem, which he believes regulates male-typical sexual behavior in nonhuman animals, might account for differences in sexual orientation. LeVay found that, out of 41 autopsied brains, a small group of cells called the third interstitial nucleus of the anterior hypothalamus (or INAH-3) was on average twice as large in heterosexual men as in either women or gay men.[62] (The language of size itself might reinforce heterocentrist values, construing women and gay men as deficient. But is bigger better, or are straight men just fatheaded?) While studies of tropical fish have shown the hypothalamus to be something that is not fixed, but instead changes with environmental conditions, LeVay mentions only the male rat, whose preoptic nucleus seems to stabilize prenatally. This suggests that LeVay is wedded to the promise of a clear and distinct natural homosexual minority.[63] *Newsweek's* report on LeVay's work was advertised with a white baby on the cover and the question, "Is This Child Gay?"[64] But, the complexity and modesty of the scientific project and its conclusions that get lost, or perverted, in the translation from scientific journals to the popular press is not the only problem.[65]

All 41 brains in LeVay's study were obtained from people who had died from complications associated with AIDS. LeVay assumed that the men in his study who reported being infected with HIV through homosexual intercourse were homosexual, and that the men who reported that the source of HIV transmission was intravenous drugs were heterosexual. The sexual orientations of the women did not interest LeVay. Of course, having homosexual sex does not mean that someone is or identifies as homosexual; one might have been paid for homosexual sex, have had it once as a youth, or perform it secretly while identifying as heterosexual, for instance. Even if the deceased had identified themselves as such, LeVay cannot infer anything about how much homosexual sex they had or desired, or how much heterosexual sex they had or desired—precisely that with which he claims the INAH-3 size correlates. LeVay tries to circumvent this problem by suggesting that the INAH-3 correlates with the direction of *either* feelings or behavior.

Further problems finding a biological basis for sexual identities arise when modern technology is considered. A woman might get a sex reassignment operation and live as a man, having heterosexual sex with women. What size might the INAH-3 region of his hypothalamus be? What of variations in sexual orientation other than object choice—such as scripted versus nonscripted sex, sex in public versus sex in private, orgasmic versus nonorgasmic sex, sex with one person versus more than one, and so on?[66] These variations seem not to concern evolutionary theorists precisely because such preferences are assumed to be less intrinsic or fundamental to our being than the gender of object choice. Variations in sexual orientation that do not revolve around sex categories are ignored, suggesting that evolutionary theorists presume and perpetuate a sex binarism, which queer theorists and postmodern feminists have analyzed as central to a disciplinary regime of heterosexuality.[67]

Studies like LeVay's take for granted a sexually desiring agent as their subject of analysis. In this framework, the INAH-3 would never be hypothesized to correlate with, for instance, the genders (or some other features) of those people who tend to be attracted to the agent. Instead, it is the subject who is thought to have a substance in his brain that directs his desire to specific others.[68] Social theorist David Halperin has pointed out that many premodern and non-Western cultures did not individuate people at the level of sexual orientation and instead assumed that sexuality was no more categorizable or innate than modern people consider dietary preferences to be.[69] From this vantage point, scientific studies looking for links between sexual orientation and biology could be questioned not only for their assumption that an individual's sexuality is directed toward a specific gender category, but for their assumption that individuals have an intrinsic component of their subjectivity that we call "sexuality" at all.

Since sexual identifications change across history, cultures, and an individual's life span, any attempt to ground an identity in nature is suspect.[70] Only relatively recently and in the West has a homosexual/heterosexual division become such a salient dichotomy for identification.[71] It has been posited that in the Mexican/Latin American system, a man's sexual identity is based on a preference for certain acts rather than on the gender of object choice.[72] The argument that one could be biologically wired for a position in a sexual categorization system that is itself culturally and historically constructed arrogantly presumes the universality of peculiarly modern and Western identities.

Attempting to establish homosexuality as biologically based is not only sociologically and scientifically undiscerning, but also politically shortsighted, since doing so will not necessarily ensure gay rights. Progay scientists like LeVay and their adherents might anticipate that, because the "unnaturalness" of homosexuality has historically been used in order to condemn it politically, scientifically establishing its "naturalness" may be what will convince homophobes to change their views. However, the attempt to secure gay rights through scientific claims about nature contains many pitfalls.[73] The arguments for a gay brain or gay gene, however well intended, are nonsensical on evolutionary terms (there is no need to assume that a human heterosexual orientation was adaptive), and asociological in their insistence that such an historically and culturally constructed category for identity could be inborn.

The hope to secure gay rights through such an argument, even if successful, has other political problems as well. Namely, it authorizes scientific knowledge to settle political disputes, as though such knowledge is value-free. It reproduces the same foundationalist logic that has historically been used against gays. It also ignores other sexual minorities (celibates, shoe fetishists, and strappers-on), leaving them in the marginalized dust until someone proves that they, too, are born that way. Positioning homosexuality as a biological orientation also ignores the ways in which biology is increasingly dissociated from the unchangeable (think of the well-funded Human Genome Project and other technologies for altering what was once considered destiny). Finally, the strategy of positioning homosexuality as a biological-minority orientation solidifies rather than dissolves the natural and normative status of heterosexuality. [74]

Learning to Live with Perversion

Scientific narratives that naturalize heterosexuality *create* reality while pretending to offer innocent descriptions of reality. The ritual enactments of the evolutionary myth of natural manhood (which, precisely because it is not real or natural or automatic, must be relentlessly rehearsed and reestablished) have defined and restricted life chances for anyone who is not a "natural" man. I suggest that we approach scientific texts the way queer theorists have approached other cultural texts. This involves embracing the instability of knowledge and identities, undermining that "organic" feeling straight men, however precariously, preserve. Evolutionary stories naturalize heterosexuality not because the "facts" of evolution simply force us to accept our soiled (heterosexual) animal natures, but because an unexamined commitment to the privileged, universal status of Western heterosexual masculinity has influenced the kind of evolutionary psychologies theorists have imagined and projected onto our past.[75] Further, the status of scientific knowledge as producer of authoritative accounts of the real conceals the politics of naturalizing heterosexuality.

In this intellectual exercise, I have not questioned the legitimacy of the theory of evolution itself (although others, creationists for instance, would), or its specific assumptions about natural selection or the genetic basis for sexual predilections. I have taken the theory of evolution on its own terms, and constructed a new interpretation of sexual behavior based on an alternative set of background assumptions. To construe evolutionary theory itself as the enemy of women and queers concedes too much to popular cultural assumptions of the evolutionary advantage of predatory heterosexual desire and the stability of scientific texts. I have employed evolutionary theory to pull the nature rug out from under straight men's feet and to undermine heterosexism and scientific authoritarianism more generally.

Queer interpretations of cultural texts destabilize straight texts, the apparent stability of which many bank on. Queer interpretations are no more biased than straight interpretations. As Seidman puts it,

In the spirit of deconstruction, queering does not mean improving upon or substituting one set of foundational assumptions and narratives for another, but leaving permanently open and contestable the assumptions and narratives that guide social analysis and assessing them in terms of multidimensional, pragmatic considerations.[76]

No story of the meaning of animal mating habits or of human evolutionary history could ever be independent of political commitments. Nondominant perspectives can point to new directions for research and to new interpretations of nature. The new stories that result have different social consequences, but they are still value-laden stories.

The belief that some sort of neutral "truth" exists and can arbitrate political conflicts is based on the tired, old distinction between knowledge and politics--one that holds up scientific knowledge as a promising foundation for moral meaning, the truth that will set us free.[77] But scientific accounts of sexuality and mating can never represent the world independent of human values. The conventional, objectivist philosophy of scientific knowledge, which presupposes a nature "out there" that we can describe neutrally, assumes that talking about birds and fish in terms saturated with human meanings masks what is going on in nature. In other words, we should beware of the panda's "thumb." (Stephen Jay Gould tells us that what appears to be a sixth digit of the giant panda is not a digit at all, but a bit of elongated bone.)[78] Feminist critics of sociobiology have condemned the use of terms like *rape*, *homosexual*, and *adultery* to describe practices of nonhuman animals, arguing that such words in a sociobiological context are "jargon" and have "possible social repercussions" and that less emotionally evocative terms should be used.[79]

While such critiques have been important for exposing the values in scientific descriptions, it is time to move beyond these critiques, since they, too, privilege certain stories on epistemological rather than political grounds—as though the "correct" politics will lead us to the "correct" story. The stories feminists privilege are not jargon- or metaphor-free; nor are they less distorted representations of nature. As Williams notes, feminists have not objected to saying that animals practice "courtship," "fasting," and "migration" (or "bonding," "friendship," etc.).[80] And while the use of the term *forced pair copulations* (rather than *rape*) might sound more technical, such terminology does not make scientific stories free of human values or social repercussions; they simply do a better job of hiding them. Perhaps we should also beware of the mallard's forced pair copulations.

Since scientific stories about human behavior are inescapably value-laden, making values more invisible only enables irresponsible storytelling. My critique acknowledges the impossibility of describing nature neutrally. Queer interpretations try to make conspicuous the values and political commitments that inform them. They also promise to undermine dominant knowledge regimes without making the same mistake of offering an impossibly innocent discourse. My alternative account of men's evolved sexual psychology is no less, and no more, a "just so story" than hetero-centrist evolutionary narratives.

Although any strategy for disrupting the dominant sexual system is risky, I am convinced that the strategy that discommodes the method of privilege legitimation is more promising than the strategy that preserves the traditional relationships between essentialism and morality.[81] In making science our bible, the traditional approach forecloses responsible dialogue over political commitments and rights for the sexual minorities whose deviance revolves around something other than having partners of the "wrong" gender. The "gay brain" approach, while it promises to mess with the minds of many homophobes who have justified their discrimination on biological grounds, fails to loosen heterosexuality from its privileged place as natural and inevitable. That approach also fails to challenge the position of science as an authoritative arbiter of political conflicts. After all, what counts as "perversion" is a matter of politics, not nature. The attempt to ground homosexuality in nature, therefore, holds less promise than a queer theory approach that undermines the naturalized sex binarism, the mythic naturalness of heterosexuality, and the authority of science altogether.

I thus have engaged evolutionary theory here not to reinstitute the hegemony of scientific discourse, but to undermine it, showing how all such scientific stories, straight and queer, have political bases and political consequences. In other words, I have not tried to set the evolutionary record straight, but to queer the evolutionary record. Exposing the hetero-centrist assumptions that have been an implicit part of evolutionary theorizing might complicate "innocent" attempts to naturalize heterosexuality and offers scientists, feminists, and queers new possibilities for theorizing. Instead of making science our bible, the queer-theory approach insists upon making conspicuous the political commitments of any knowledge production process.

With an understanding of scientific texts as cultural texts, men might find it harder to perform in the mode of *Homo habitus*—that is, feeling instinctually like a caveman. In the next chapter, I offer a means for men to think differently about both scientific stories and masculinity with an attentiveness to textuality. In essence, I suggest that men evolve from *Homo habitus* to *Homo textual*.

5

HOMO TEXTUAL

A MISSING LINK BETWEEN
SCIENCE AND CULTURE

Popularity and Reality

The popularity of the caveman narrative today tells us that men are feeling angry, sexually deprived, and powerless. It also tells us that science remains an authoritative answer in regards to our bodies and political arrangements. It tells us that bodies are increasingly seen as the originator of culture, rather than vice versa. It further tells us that political arrangements are seen as the expressions of biological essences rather than the institutional forces that find their expression in lived bodies.

We can see not only science but masculinity differently once we understand the social origins of ideas and the effects those ideas have on society and individuals' feelings and behaviors. Social, and not merely scientific, reasons have enabled the success of human behavior and evolution (HBE) discourse. The caveman ethos offers men a scientifically endorsed form of macho defiance. The caveman mystique lets men off the hook for a number of reasons: first, because science is like a God, blind submission to which gives some men relief and even great pleasure; second, because any authority is less challenging than autonomy (the word of science over and above an independent, personal capacity to make moral decisions); and third, because the institutionalization of feminist gender norms requires the sublimation of hostilities and aggressions for which women have been normally and acceptably the object.

HBE ideas have become popular, then, because they meet social needs and expectations and carry the cultural purchase of science. They then get implemented by policy makers and through social institutions, which further establish specific models of masculine identity and norms for behavior. They are appealing not because they are so compelling scientifically, but because any scientific explanation has appeal, especially when it reinforces how men want to see themselves. Explanations of men's putatively innate drives might be particularly appealing to economically or racially privileged men who cannot as easily fall back on environmentalist excuses for "bad boy" behavior, such as the conditions of poverty. At the same time, as I have argued, evolutionary narratives might appeal to men from lower economic echelons for other reasons—namely, as the one way they can feel manly in a stratified society that put them behind other men and many women. HBE's explanatory power, then, has more to do with the way it meets personal needs and social expectations than with its scientific accuracy.

Although we can explain the popularity of the caveman story, there are several reasons for questioning evolutionary theory and its authority as a source of information about who men really are. I have argued that it's too simple to observe behavioral patterns and, if universal or explicable by evolutionary theory, conclude that those patterns must be expressions of evolutionary psychology. But what about the men who feel or act like cavemen? How do we know that their feelings and behaviors do not come from their genes or an evolved sexual psychology? As chapter 3 disclosed, cultural norms and knowledge affect a habitus, a bodily demeanor with physical habits and tastes. Consider, by way of analogy, another discourse that affected gendered experiences of physicality. Victorian women *really did* pass out on fainting couches and *really were* weaker than men, but we now understand that they were living out the stereotype their society had assigned to them. Such social stereotypes and the self-understandings they generate are embodied. Today many men really do feel like cavemen, but it's too simple a step to assume that feelings reveal an inner biological essence.

Chapter 4 explained the ways in which professional science gets blended with its popular versions (or distortions) in the mass media. It also revealed that the topics of HBE research reflect common cultural assumptions about gender and sexuality. Sometimes these chosen topics appear to be deadlocked with an imaginary feminist antiscience rival with whom HBE scholars compete to explain specific problems like rape and harassment. Evolutionary theorists commonly study that which makes men seem sexually vigorous. If evolutionary explanations for nondominant male behaviors were offered, those outside scientific circles probably would not hear about them.

HBE theorists could just as easily come up with an evolutionary account that explains, for instance, impotence. Arguably more common in men than raping, impotence might have been adaptive in the environment of evolutionary adaptedness (the hunting and gathering part of our human history; hereafter, EEA). An HBE theorist could reason that during stressful times a man wouldn't have been able to get an erection, and that this might have served men well in terms of reproductive success, as stressful times would have been the same times that made a baby's survival difficult. This would mean that men who were not impotent would have mated no matter how dangerous the survival conditions. Those men's children would have been less likely to survive, whereas the impotent men and their children would have had better reproductive success, thereby ensuring the perpetuation of an impotence-reaction psychology. But instead of stressing the evolved psychological reaction of impotence today (particularly among men who are stressed by their jobs or with few possibilities of employment), men's preferences for women with slim waists and other features that reveal men to be virile, aggressively heterosexual creatures are priorities for HBE theorizing and its popular promotion.

HBE scientists research specific questions that cultural conditions generated. HBE scholars notice women bought and sold as property by men in various parts of the world. If feminists discuss that as an example of patriarchy, HBE scholars can say, "But, you see, evolutionary theory can explain why this happens!" Similarly, if feminists talk about economic inequalities that affect women's mate preferences, HBE scholars can say, "But, you see, evolutionary theory can explain why women are poorer than men!" Such logic fails to account for sexist practices as well as feminist change. It also loses track of the potential for collective transformation for the liberation of humanity, in the spirit of Enlightenment values of human rights. As such, HBE is unsavory; it is not the best myth for a sustainable and just future.

HBE scholars and their enthusiasts see evolution explaining our preoccupation with sex and relationships. They notice our sex-obsessed society in advertisements alluding to sex, video stores selling images of it, and people talking about it, reading about how to get more of it, and going to therapy to improve it. But current conditions, even if their effects are nearly universal, cannot serve as uncomplicated evidence of human nature or the expression of evolved sexual psychologies. That our culture today is awash in sex cannot serve as evidence that this is our human nature, a psychology that was adaptive back in the EEA. Sex has a new and different place in our world than it had just a few generations ago. Some would even argue that sex itself has replaced religion as the new sacred.[1] Once we understand what Steven Seidman calls "the sociohistorical transformation of bodies, desires, and intimacies or 'sex' into 'sexuality,'" then we see just how uncritical and ahistorical HBE theory's approach to sex is.[2] HBE theory treats sex as a natural fact, as an inner force we must know and either fulfill or control.

There is also the ambiguity of HBE scholars' professional distance from political issues and their simultaneous concern about social problems. As I revealed in chapter 2, HBE scholars quite often have an ideological investment—even when they say that they'll leave social change up to the policy makers. They and their enthusiasts are as invested in combating the problems of pollution, overpopulation, and violations of basic human rights as the next person. They also are invested in science being the master discipline that can show us how, or at least how not, to solve these problems. And I don't blame them for these investments. But for many average Joes, "science" replaces (or supplements) "the Creator" in basic arguments about men's roles, problems, and rights. So, in the current cultural context in which scientific ideas are pursued, funded, and deemed important, HBE ideas hold sway not because they are simply solid scientific ideas, but because they speak to intense social and moral concerns. HBE ideas carry an often unquestioned scientific authority their popularizers use to persuade the public about policy matters and personal relationships.

In *Genes, Mind and Culture*, Charles Lumsden and Edward Wilson argue that we urgently need evolutionary knowledge to save humans and the entire planet.[3] A social engineering program can accomplish this so that cultural constraints would encourage ideals like cooperation and curb aggression and other values that are, at least in our current global society, self-destructive. Note Lumsden and Wilson, "A sufficient knowledge of genes and mental development can lead to the development of a form of social engineering that changes not only the likelihood of the outcome but the deepest feelings about right and wrong, in other words, the ethical precepts themselves."[4] If this is true, then incorrect or ideologically troubling knowledge of genes can also change feelings about right and wrong. It is precisely because I believe Lumsden and Wilson that I insist we use great caution as we consider the claims of evolutionary science. Even if the evolutionary claims about heterosexual male desire and aggression turn out to be incorrect, they will have nevertheless changed feelings about right and wrong—and not necessarily in the way prominent HBE scholars like Wilson would have hoped.

Evolutionary Theory and Scientific Certainty

Despite the cultural authority of the science of human nature, HBE theory is hardly an exact science. HBE theorists imagine what our ancestors were like and test some hypotheses, which can often be validated by today's norms. But the behaviors, feelings, and desires that evolutionary scholars take an interest in are only presumed to have a genetic base. A trait cannot be human nature if it does not have a genetic component. And so far there is no proof of a gene for a desire for big breasts, or a gene for promiscuity. HBE scholars think the existence of such a genetic component makes sense, but no one has actual scientific evidence for it.

To illustrate just how uncertain HBE research is, let us examine David Buss' mate-selection study. Though there are many academic research papers in HBE, Buss' serves as an interesting example because he is considered an authority by his own academic peers and is widely cited in the field. He is also cited by many of the popularizers of HBE thought. Buss himself has appeared on many news programs and is also cited approvingly in Steven Rhoads's *Taking Sex Differences Seriously*, the book about why feminist changes are futile.[5] Buss argues that because a behavior is (somewhat) universal and is in line with selectionist reasoning, then it's plausible that the behavior is part of human nature. He tells readers in his *Evolution of Desire*, an engaging book written for a wide audience, that his cross-cultural study found the predicted sex differences in human mating preferences universally.[6] Internationally, men tend to value physical attractiveness and youth in a mate more than women, who are more likely than men to prioritize resources in a mate. Reading about the study, one would think that all men prioritize good looks in a mate above all else, and that looks don't matter to women at all.

However, if you go back and read Buss' boring old academic article, published in *Behavioral and Brain Sciences* in 1989, you will see that the picture is more complicated than that, and he readily admits to several limitations of his study.[7] For example, he did not have a random sample. He also concedes that self-reports are limited and must be checked by other studies. (A man may say beauty in a woman is highly important, for instance, but then will actually pair up with someone who is rich and not very good looking.) Buss also notes that male and female preferences overlap significantly. Not only do women also express a preference for good looks in a mate (just not as strongly as men), both men and women prefer, first and foremost, kindness and understanding in their mates.

Another limitation, which Buss does not discuss, is his study's use of unconditional rather than conditional tests. The former type of study, as in this case, looks at preferences in mating without controlling for possible determinants (such as economic status). Thus, we do not know whether or not a nonevolutionary reason accounts for the preference because it was not tested for. So while the results do not contradict a selectionist argument, the sex differences expressed in desirable qualities in a mate also are consistent with women's subordinate economic position—which would also predict that women would value a man who is a good financial prospect over one who is great looking.

Studies like this only show that there is an average sex difference in preference in many cultures, but, interestingly, not as extreme a difference as we might expect if selection designed men to prioritize good looks. Buss' study revealed that men's preferences for good looks are, on average, only 11 percent stronger than women's in any given country. A distinction must be made between men's expressing a slightly stronger preference for good looks than women do in a given culture and the Darwinian theoretical prediction that men carry sex-linked genes for mate preferences due to sex differences in reproductive strategies. The hypothesis from selectionist reasoning would be that there are sex differences in desires for mates, not that only a majority of men would have such preferences or that men's preferences for good looks are just slightly stronger than women's preferences for the same thing. Buss ignores the intragroup difference, and thus the failure of the evolutionary theoretical prediction.

Moreover, Buss does not explain the variation across cultures. For instance, women in Nigeria and India placed a greater value on good looks than did Japanese men. While it's true that Nigerian men placed an even greater value on looks than Nigerian women, and that Japanese men placed greater value on looks than Japanese women, selectionist reasoning would not predict, and cannot account for, the variation between men in different countries—which is sometimes even greater than the variation between men and women in a particular place. Similarly, while women ranked being a good financial prospect higher than their countrymen did, Indian men ranked it higher than women in Finland, Great Britain, Norway, Spain, and Australia. But Buss focuses instead on a statistically significant difference between men and women in a given country, conveniently ignoring the significant number of men who do not rank the attributes the selectionist argument would predict as high as some women did.

This study of cross-cultural sex differences in mate preferences does not decompose the data to show, statistically, the source of the differences among men, the differences between cultures, or the differences between men and women in a given culture. Given this, noting that, cross-culturally, men express a slightly stronger preference for good looks in a mate than women do hardly establishes a sex-linked genetic connection or disputes sociological explanations for such observable sex differences. A statistically significant difference is not necessarily an evolutionarily significant difference.

In 1990, Buss and a long list of coauthors published a follow-up study in the *Journal of Cross-Cultural Psychology*, which did crunch the numbers in a way that would show what amount of the variation in preferences is due to culture and, on the other hand, to sex.[8] They found that across 31 different mate characteristics, only 2.4 percent of the total variance in preferences can be accounted for by whether the preference came from a man or a woman. Culture accounted for an average of 14 percent of the variance.[9] When it came to good looks, 7 percent of the variance in preference for this mate characteristic was due to sex. Of course, even if sex accounts for a small amount of the variance in mate selection preferences, we still do not know whether that is biology acting on men and women or something else.

Decades ago, just after E. O. Wilson's *Sociobiology* was published, Stephen Jay Gould argued that nongenetic explanations could still be provided for many of the same behaviors evolutionary arguments explained.[10] Gould noted that sociobiology employs three strategies to show that a behavior has a genetic base: first, if a behavior is universal; second, if it's seen in the animal kingdom and can be explained in Darwinian terms;

and finally, if there is a plausible explanation of how the behavior would have been adaptive.[11] The HBE field has grown since the time Gould made this assessment. However, popularizers and enthusiasts of evolutionary explanations still need to be reminded that a behavior is not necessarily genetic simply because it's universal, because animals do it, or because we can think of why a behavior would have been adaptive. A plausible argument that a behavior would have been adaptive does not mean that other plausible, nongenetic arguments must necessarily be wrong. Men's desires and behaviors could be explained differently and with equal plausibility.

The fact is that we don't really know what the facts are. Evolutionary claims about human desires and behaviors can only be speculative. Evolutionary science is still being appraised and debated. For this reason, basing our self-knowledge, our actions, and/or our ethical prescriptions on such a flimsy view of human nature is unwise. HBE is a source of interesting and possibly useful information, but so are the insights of many other fields, which HBE will not be able to overtake or incorporate into any kind of grand synthesis.

But despite—or perhaps because of—its speculative character, evolutionary thinking can be seductive. It is all too easy to come up with a persuasive argument about how something could have been adaptive. For this very reason I even considered my own hypothetical version of the Sokal Hoax (for more on this, see chapter 1). It would go something like this: Is there an evolutionary basis for the social pattern of men preferring physically beautiful but dumb women, and avoiding women who are smart, while women choose smart men over dim-witted men? Evolutionary theory would predict that women would value male partners who are capable of resource provisioning, which would be correlated with smarts or brain size. Since women in the EEA, who showed a preference for men with big brains, would have had greater reproductive success, male ancestors with big brains had greater reproductive success as well.

But, given the above, how is it that women *also* have large brains? Is that simply an evolutionary "accident" that unavoidably resulted from the pattern of natural selection for men with big brains? My answer would be yes. Indeed, I might further suggest, we see here an answer to our earlier question about men preferring dumb-but-pretty women: this is an outcome of the competitive nature of natural selection. As a result of women's evolutionary preference for smart men, women also got smarter, but, after a time, ancestral men realized that as smart women chose their sexual partners they would make more accurate judgments about which men were, in fact, big brained, and so those middling-brained men set in motion a counterevolutionary strategy to maximize their own chances for reproductive success. They began to choose women who were physically attractive, but who were also not so smart. They began to choose, in a word, cavebimbos.

We can find much evidence for the selectionist argument that men avoid smart women and seek beautiful, relatively stupid ones. After all, men across cultures experience smart women as unattractive—threatening, even—and many of the most famous smart women never married and were not regarded as beautiful: Susan B. Anthony, Sarah Grimke, Gertrude Stein, Jane Addams. On the other hand, human history is filled with examples of beautiful women who were married to men and who never had careers or intellectual expression whatsoever. This cultural pattern of mate-selection preference is universal, as is the fact that women do not do as well as men in fields requiring strong intellect. Just look at women in the Middle East. Some might question how women there would fare if more of them were actually allowed to go to school, but then the fact that far more men than women get formal educations is consistent with the argument that men are in greater competition for women who seek men with big brains.

This is not to suggest that women are *far less* intelligent than men or have brains *much* smaller than men's. Many scientific studies reveal that women's abilities in math and science are lower than men's, but not grossly so. Women do indeed have large brains, too, though the large human female brain is not an adaptation. A woman's large brain is nature's way of being efficient—like male nipples or the female orgasm!

I like to imagine that I could get my evolutionary theory published, just like Alan Sokal got his bogus social constructionist reading of physics published. I would expect my theory to be taken seriously because it supports the significance of evolution in shaping sex-specific preferences and explains an observable phenomenon. Of course, if my article did get published in *Evolution and Human Behavior,* I would expose the journal's editors as having failed to consult the relevant cultural studies scholars whose expertise on sex inequality, gender identity, and the embodiment of gender ideology would have cast doubt on my fraudulent claims. I would explain that those scholars would have pointed out why married women historically did not get to have careers or otherwise express themselves intellectually. Those scholars would also point to the many ways in which our definitions of female beauty coincide with patriarchal power relationships. In the meantime, television shows would likely feature the story, "Why Gentlemen Prefer Dumb Blondes." Of course, the men's magazines would declare, "Knuckle Draggers Unite! Science Proves Men Genetically Can't Deal with Smart Women."

Evolutionary Insights for a Change

As I showed in chapter 2, HBE scholars and their popularizers often promise that HBE theory is important, not for uniting knuckle draggers, but for changing individual behaviors and improving society. However, they do not actually provide examples of anyone changing their behavior based on evolutionary insight (save for Richard Alexander, who speaks, modestly, only for himself).[12] Robin Baker's *Sperm Wars* is illustrative, and we benefit from a new introduction to the 2006 edition of his book.[13] In that introduction, Baker explains that he received many letters after the 1996 edition was read widely and that these letters were from everyday readers "reassured" about, mainly, the infidelity or promiscuity they had experienced but, until *Sperm Wars*, had not been able to explain.[14] Baker does not mention that the readers changed their ways; indeed, there is reason to believe that they felt reassured precisely because the evolutionary explanation allowed them to avoid responsibility for their actions.

Although Baker says in his preface—in reference to rape, specifically—that "the first step in dealing with antisocial behavior is to understand it—and that and nothing else is the aim of all my interpretations,"[15] his concluding chapter contains the statement,

> Some things, of course, will never change. Nothing—short of castration, brain surgery or hormone implants—can remove a person's subconscious urge to have as many grandchildren as they can. So, nothing will remove a man's subconscious urge to have as many children with as many women as his genes and circumstances will allow.[16]

On the one hand, Baker tells us we must understand men's nature in order to solve problems like rape; moreover, we do not ethically have to allow men's nature to express itself. On the other hand, we must understand that male nature will never change.

Similarly, another HBE book marketed to a wide audience, *Making Sense of Sex*, written by the husband–wife team of David Barash and Eve Lipton, insists that

> women and men will maximize their power to choose when they have maximized their understanding of who they are, that is, who is making those choices—or, in Reinhold Niebuhr's (author of *The Serenity Prayer*) terms, when they have acquired the wisdom to know the difference between what cannot be changed and what can.[17]

Apparently, evolutionary science grants us the wisdom to know the difference. At the same time, in that same chapter, the authors warn, "Although we are confident that biology generates sex differences, we are leery of deriving societal prescriptions from scientific descriptions, even the evolutionary ones we so fervently espouse."[18] On the one hand, we must know about biological sex differences because they are consequential; on the other hand, they do not mean to imply the differences are of consequence.

This same chapter includes a quote by feminist Betty Friedan as its epigraph, to emphasize the authors' sympathy with challenging gender norms. On the one hand, change is possible; on the other hand we are supposed to understand that some things about male and female nature cannot be changed. Moreover, on the one hand, we should study evolution for its own sake, just to know the truth. On the other hand, evolutionary insights have implications for many interested parties, including social scientists, women's liberationists, and policy makers.

HBE fails to deliver on either of its main promises, however contradictory these promises are. First, it fails to help policy makers change society and individuals to change themselves in ways that counter what they say is human nature. Second, it fails to stay out of political debates. So, while there is a hope that the truth revealed by evolutionary science applied to humans will help us solve social problems like oppressive violence, theories from evolutionary science have not actually spurred individual or policy changes to constrain that violence.

While HBE scholars stress people's abilities to free themselves from genetic tyranny, to decide what ought to be independent of what HBE scholarship says is the case, they are incredibly reluctant to answer the question of just which aspects of human nature can change and which cannot. And more significant, they do not give examples of which policies or institutional arrangements should change in light of evolutionary insight into human nature. For example, is getting married a good idea? Is expecting to have a monogamous relationship a dumb idea? Despite HBE scholars' emphasis on controlling our passions, HBE thought stresses the power of biology and our lack of control. Even if our behaviors can be controlled or managed, the message is that our desires and inner feelings cannot. Men can avoid moral responsibility for their desires or "drives" if they manage not to act on them.

The message from evolutionary scholars is consistent: know yourself, in the evolutionary sense, so that you can become the master of your life rather than a slave to your genes. But in the end, the maxim "know thyself" becomes its own end. They do not spend time telling us what "knowing" that men lust after women does for us. Whether they blame their DNA or the devil, many men already think this about themselves. So, why is it more meaningful to think of oneself in the terms of evolutionary science? How does evolutionary knowledge help a couple deal with something particularly painful in their relationship, such as a secret affair or pornography addiction?

Apparently, the appeal lies in "demystifying" sex differences and little else. But still, we might ask, in what sense are sex differences demystified if one man remains faithfully devoted to the same woman for decades, as Charles Darwin himself did, while another man cheats on his wife the moment their marriage begins? How are sex differences demystified when one man marries for a woman's intelligence or sense of humor while another man gets himself a dim-witted trophy wife? How are sexual relations demystified if one man is addicted to online pornography while another feels that consuming such materials would spoil his sexual relationships with women? How are sexual relations demystified when three men gang rape a drunk woman, but a fourth man calls the police? HBE theory fails to provide any real insight into the motivations and moral choices that distinguish men from one another.

Some HBE theorists caution people not to take ethical prescriptions from their theories. They urge us not to turn *is* into *ought*. In a 1997 interview, Richard Dawkins is clearly frustrated and irritated that he and his colleagues have so often been asked about their research being in bed with conservative political goals when he says,

> [T]he opponents of sociobiology are too stupid to understand the distinction between what one says about the way the world is, scientifically, and

the way it ought to be politically. They look at what we say about natural selection, as a scientific theory for what is, and they assume that anybody who says that so and so is the case, must therefore be advocating that it ought to be the case in human politics. They cannot see that it is possible to separate one's scientific beliefs about what is the case in nature from one's political beliefs about what ought to be in human society.[19]

Notice that Dawkins describes the *opponents* of sociobiology as too stupid to distinguish descriptions of the world from prescriptions for the world. Yet the *proponents* of sociobiology are often equally incapable of making this distinction as well. HBE ideas appeal to people who are foundationalist and who want easy answers to their personal problems and existential questions. They also appeal to those who want to be let off the hook for their feelings and desires. HBE scholars like Dawkins neglect to scold men who enthusiastically embrace their work for the ethical implications they presume it has. Indeed, HBE theorists are not particularly vocal about their enthusiasts' misuses of their work. Instead, they seem to be far more upset about their critics' mischaracterizations of their work, a point I will return to later in this chapter.

Dawkins is surely correct that many people out there are far less sophisticated in their views than he is. Moreover, some people who oppose biological explanations only do so precisely because they are as foundationalist as everyone else: they don't want us to see human nature as bad, or male nature as sexually aggressive because they think that would imply we would need to accept it ethically. Yet, it is far too simplistic to view, and even advocate, a perspective that scientists simply and innocently describe "what is" independent of values and background assumptions. After all, their view of *what is* is influenced by *what already has been*, which is itself influenced by *what people have thought ought to be*—which was influenced by *what people thought was*, which was influenced by *what people thought ought to be*, which … and so on.

HBE scholars also accuse their academic rivals of insisting that biology does not influence people. For instance, Malcolm Potts and Roger Short, in their textbook *Ever Since Adam and Eve: The Evolution of Human Sexuality*, declare, "A newborn child is not a blank sheet of emotional and behavioural paper."[20] But from there they leap to cultural universals serving as evidence that something is an evolved biological predisposition. Indeed, Buss takes his finding *cross-culturally* that men are the sex with a stronger preference for good looks in a mate as practically incontrovertible evidence that those preferences are evolved psychological dispositions. How do we know what women would desire if they could afford to desire beauty over resources, or if men had to rely on women to get by financially? What about the effects of consumer culture in shaping men's desires for sex with women who look a certain way?

But as soon as we ask feminist questions that challenge a biological explanation of such sex differences, HBE scholars start pointing fingers, saying that it's feminists who are naive and extremist. For example, Steven Pinker accuses feminists (except for the ones writing critiques of feminism, whom he cites approvingly) of insisting all gender inequities are cultural rather than biological when, according to Pinker, these inequities are caused by both biological and environmental factors.[21] HBE theorists like Pinker routinely fault their sociological and feminist critics for presumably suggesting that humans are a "blank slate" (what Pinker titled his 2002 book on the modern denial of human nature), as though we do not pay attention to biology at all. With this assumption, Pinker and his ilk expose themselves as decades behind in their knowledge of social science and humanities scholarship.[22]

Despite his initial insistence that biology *and* culture determine sex-linked behaviors, Pinker goes on to emphasize biology over culture. As an example, he uses the much discussed John/Joan case in which an American boy was castrated during a botched circumcision and, thereafter, was raised as a girl. That this child grew up and eventually sought a sex reassignment operation to live as a man is evidence, Pinker says, that gendered preferences in toys, dress, and so on are biologically based. Yet this only reveals Pinker's naïveté about how gender operates. For instance, Pinker pays no attention to the fact that little Joan's parents knew they'd given birth to, and begun raising, John, a factor that was bound to affect how they (and the doctors) treated the child.[23]

Pinker also seems to think that if we see sex segregation in the workplace, it indicates that women choose, based on their biologically based skills, to go into fields that just happen to make less money than the fields that men choose, based on their biologically based skills. The skills he's referring to include men's better performance on spatial relations tests relative to women, and women's superior performance remembering locations of objects. However, as I mentioned in chapter 4, we see quite a bit of variation in skills within a sex category, with some women doing better than some men, and vice-versa. How is it that such skills are presumed to be based in evolution? If a particular skill was needed for men to survive, wouldn't an overwhelming majority of them by now have it? And if cavewomen's roles were so different from their male counterparts, why then would so many women have comparable if not superior skill in the same areas as men?

In the end, Pinker says—quite erroneously—that feminists want everyone to be the same, whereas he is willing to respect the choices women make to do different jobs. I wonder if Pinker is willing to "respect" the "choices" made by African American and Latino men to go into jobs that pay less than the jobs white men tend to hold. Certainly he would not see patterns of race-based segregation in the labor force as evidence that men of color have innately different skills and interests than white men. But with sex differences, he sees biology—and specifically, differences in evolved minds—at work. I am not disputing Pinker in order to assert that it's exclusively culture or environment, but to ask: How do we know? Have we really had enough time since the days when women were not even allowed to be educated at universities alongside men? Have we really had enough time since the Civil Rights Act of 1964 criminalized discrimination on the basis of sex (among other things) in employment, public facilities, and government? Are we sure that the different "choices" women make really are choices based in sex-linked dispositions?

Most outrageous is Pinker's assertion that he is willing to value both men and women for the unique things they offer to one another. Women may be complaining about being second-class citizens, but from what Pinker calls "a gene's point of view," men and women make a complementary pair of equal value.[24] This assertion echoes the conservative Christian sentiment, so often expressed in response to feminist demands for equal opportunity, that men and women are already equal in God's eyes. In this way, HBE scholarship fails to offer anything beyond the traditional religious view of the complementarity of the sexes. Despite HBE scholars' contention that people don't like their work because they are offended by the threat to religion they think HBE ideas imply, HBE theory is a secular version of many traditional Christian ideas and, therefore, is not particularly progressive.

Pinker is in such a competition with his "tabula rasa" social scientist nemeses that when he approvingly mentions feminist gains in our culture, he attributes this to "the inexorable logic of the expanding moral circle, which led also to the abolition of despotism, slavery, feudalism, and racial segregation."[25] I get it: when men buy and sell women like chattel, this reveals the hold biology has on men since the cave days; when men honor women as peers with the same property rights, this is due to ethical choices made by humans who overcame their biological original sin. The message is that today's (altered) society is more equitable than a society of humans in the EEA.

Let us return to the issue of policy and other applications of the important insights HBE scholars promise they offer for bettering society. Pinker and others in HBE continue to assert the importance of their view of biology on the grounds that their views will be helpful. But if we look at gains made for women's human rights in the world today, we really cannot credit HBE scholarship for fostering these gains. If more women can read and write, can vote and hold political office, can support their children, can get medical care, and can leave men who beat and rape them, I am quite sure we have feminists to thank. These feminists have made the legal, policy, and personal changes possible without regard for theories of biological versus cultural influences on men's and women's behavior. And yet, HBE scholars continue to defend their position as though feminists will get it wrong and not help women if they do not understand the biological causes of sexist behaviors and institutional arrangements. Even if both nature and nurture play a role in determining how men treat women, policy can only effect outcomes, short of genetic engineering, by changing *social* outcomes—in other words, by social engineering.

Beyond the Grand Narrative of Science

The Caveman Mystique has shown the significance of the role of scientific discourse in authoring, and authorizing, male identity in a secular age. Scientific narratives about male biology may be comforting to some men, and may allow them to avoid responsibility for certain behaviors or feelings. Indeed, evolution has become a grand narrative that offers both a catchall explanation of "bad boy" behaviors and, sometimes, presents a path to moral redemption.

Separating out claims about human nature from how we want humans to behave does not go far enough. Marlene Zuk, the feminist evolutionary theorist who studies the sexual behavior of nonhuman animals, finds a way out of the dilemma of the social/political stereotypes that influence evolutionary interpretations of human and animal nature by claiming that nature is impartial.[26] Zuk told a graduate-school friend, who had asked how she reconciled her feminist commitments with her particular scientific interests,

> I can do what I do because nature is witless, in the sense of being impartial. Feminist points of view can help us look at science from a different angle, but they will never be able to change nature, something for which we can all be grateful.[27]

This may be the case, but we must also attend to the places where nature is or becomes what we (ever so partially) said it was. The idea of nature's impartiality has fueled political and moral arguments. Our interpretations of nature have served as a falsely neutral foundation upon which to base gender identity and political claims. These interpretations are value-laden, not neutral or innocent.

Both civil and academic duties demand truth telling. But the best truth we can tell is that there is no universal truth on which an entire community, or all parties in an argument, can hang their respective hats.[28] We cannot be freed from contingency or politics; we cannot have a grand narrative of human nature or a stabilized truth. John Michael, author of *Anxious Intellects*, explains that—far from giving us a crisis in morals or the end of community—such an acknowledgment is "a continuation of the West's best traditions and the point from which any ethically serious consideration of values or judgment or community must take its departure."[29] We must demand not only better science from the HBE theorists, but a better understanding of science in our culture at large.

If we see science as a legitimate but limited discipline, then we cannot see it as a religion. We cannot see HBE scholars as a salvation army. Science studies, including this book, dislodges the absolute authority science has enjoyed both in the public eye and in the ivory tower. But winning the science wars is not about getting rid of science. It means admitting the limitations of scientific work, and making room for other experts. It means altering the status of science without obliterating science or the hope for a better society.

Beyond the Science Wars

In chapter 1, I suggested that science studies scholars have been put on the defensive, and thus feel we have to be extraordinarily careful about the claims we're making about science. But I hope that I have shown that social scientists and humanities scholars have something authoritative to say about gender, sexuality, and the body, and that scientists could stand to be more careful in their analyses of sexuality and gender, as well as in their comments on ethics and social change. So while scientists have been insisting that the journals publishing political critiques of science get a scientist to review those articles, feminist cultural studies scholars have yet to insist that they be called upon when evolutionary scholars start explaining rape, sexual harassment, and male sexual promiscuity. *We* know more about how gender and sexuality work in society than most scientists do. I want to shift the terms of the science wars debate, from questioning the right of science studies scholars to comment on science to questioning the right of scientists to comment on complex cultural practices.

By insisting that scientists can and should be the most authoritative voice about ethics and democracy in contemporary culture, both HBE scholars and, significantly, their supporters in the popular press have exemplified and fueled a key tension in the science wars. The idea that science has the most authority on human nature and, therefore, on either gender or on ethics and democracy, is dangerous in a foundationalist cultural context. We can discard the grand narrative that science leads to moral progress while making room for scientists to be a voice for democracy and human rights. Scientists cannot have this voice on the false innocence of being neutral, objective scholars. Both scientists and humanities scholars can help people navigate moral debates, but neither can offer universal knowledge.

As chapter 2 made clear, many of the HBE theorists in the field today continue a long tradition of insisting that science should contribute to the common good (for example, by being involved in policy discussions). Ironically, science studies is considered the enemy of science in the science wars, but also wants science to contribute to the common good. The political movements of the 1960s helped start science studies, asking questions about nuclear energy, environmental destruction, and the negative effects of some technologies.[30] Precisely because of this link between political movements and science studies, Sokal and his comrades would have us believe that scholars engaged in the cultural studies of science think we can make up whatever we want about nature because it's all a social construction and that no standards of rigor apply in science studies. But I do not suggest that one can make up whatever one wants about nature or the world. Nor do I argue that culture or environment determines everything about who we are. HBE scholars themselves do not simply describe *what is*—and that does not mean they might as well throw in the towel.

As I have shown, HBE scholarship and its popular reception teeter between the vision of science as pursuing truth for its own sake (without regard for perceived social or political ramifications) and the vision of science as a guide to social policy and the moral life. Ullica Segerstråle argues that the science wars have been fought by progressives, on each side, who want science to be devoid of ideologies, which they suppose contaminate science—and hence are not antiscience.[31] Interestingly, the science wars—particularly as characterized by Paul Gross and Norman Levitt—have revealed that scientists want their claims of truth to be used to counter false claims that rationalize the unjust practices of those in power.[32] Science studies scholars, in suggesting that even scientific truth claims are themselves embedded in power relations and ideological assumptions, have merged truth and power. This left progressive scientists like Gross and Levitt—for whom, according to Segerstråle, "objective facts were important as *moral* arguments"—nervous that "any threat to the authority of science would undermine its strength as a political weapon."[33] Donna Haraway is well known for making the very argument that science is ideological at some level.[34] Recognizing that truth and power are not separable is not antiscience, nor does it mean one can make things up. Rather, we make claims we recognize as contingent, humble, and partial truths.[35]

To be fair, science studies scholars also focus on the popularization of scientific claims, rather than the scientific research itself, sometimes without making this entirely clear. I believe this explains why Gross and Levitt are so angry with feminist critics of science. They site the feminist science studies critique of the representation of the sperm as aggressive and the egg as passive in the process of fertilization. Gross and Levitt point out that while feminists critique the aggressive, competitive sperm as an example of value-laden knowledge, many scientists had already been acknowledging the egg's more active role in fertilization for decades. Feminists criticize the average portrayal—as it appears on television, in the science museum, and in what parents tell their children.

Such criticism, and ultimately transformation, of lay knowledge concerning human fertilization is crucial to a feminist project. On a visit to the Museum of Man in San Diego in the late 1990s, I saw an exhibit on human fertilization with precisely the description that Gross would have us believe does not circulate in our culture.[36] The text that accompanied the exhibit's stunning photos gave the sperm, linguistically, all the agency while describing the egg as the passive receptor of the aggressive sperm. Surely as a scientist who does know that the sperm do not have all the agency in the process of fertilization, someone like Gross would be even more likely than most to notice such a bogus account as the one I chanced upon in the Museum of Man.

What I find disturbing is that Gross and Levitt do not share their feminist colleagues' concerns with such misrepresentations of accepted scientific wisdom. They care more about showing that scientists aren't the worst of the lot, that scientists are more progressive. Yes, critics must be careful to direct their criticism at the correct targets. However, Gross and Levitt could and should be just as concerned with the grave and consequential deformations of scientific knowledge outside academic circles. And scientists could pay closer attention to what becomes of scientific work. They could, in short, pay attention to popularization. Scientists cannot hide behind the excuse that "that's a distortion of my work." They must begin to notice the political climate of their work, beyond Dawkins' "don't turn my *is* into *ought*" caveat.

Scientists could attend, whether or not they believe that science is value-laden, to the overall truth effects of their work in our culture. I have shown that many nonscientists take up scientific ideas. Why aren't the HBE popularizers on the defensive? Who is calling them to task for not being experts? If only *Muscle and Fitness* and other popular magazines were as careful as science studies scholars are about getting the science right. Indeed, it would do far more to save the reputation of scientists doing work on people to publish volumes critiquing not humanities scholars for being postmodern in their philosophy of science, but instead critiquing the far less sophisticated endorsements of their views published in popular magazines.

In further defending the authority of science against critiques by other academics, while understandable for scientists to do especially if they feel some criticism is being misdirected at them, those scientists only further cement the authoritative status of science, which propels the problem of its misuses in popular culture. A more productive way to intervene in the science wars might be to explain how and when popularizers of science and their consumers get science wrong. Instead of writing *Higher Superstition,* scientists like Gross and Levitt wishing to defend science could write a book criticizing the lack of rigor in the popular press called

Low-Brow Science Cults; and instead of Noretta Koertge's *A House Built on Sand: Exposing Postmodernist Myths about Science,* they might write a book called *Exposing Naive Endorsements of Science.*[37] As Steve Fuller notes (in the context of the Sokal Hoax), physicists should "turn their efforts at remediation on admiring New Agers, policy makers, and social scientists whose misunderstandings of physics are often as egregious as those of the STS (science and technology studies) critics."[38] The science wars have not been played out between those in the popular press who get evolutionary theory wrong in their enthusiastic attempt to spread the word of HBE scholarship. Rather, the science wars have been unfortunate fights between academics.

In his book *Anxious Intellects,* John Michael argues convincingly that the science wars are a symptom of the broader problem of resource scarcity in post-Cold War academia.[39] Due to the demands of the competitive marketplace in which students, and universities, find themselves, universities are now under increased pressure to give students competitive credentials and cultivate scholars who conduct research that has some direct relevance for business, technology, or communities—in other words, research that is not "pure." Given this, HBE scholars deserve credit for pursuing something they truly believe in. After all, they're not serving as experts on food additives or nuclear power, which Michael notes scientists do more frequently in the contemporary academic milieu.[40]

HBE scholars have been under fire from leftist academics and activists, and have often felt dismayed that their political intentions are so drastically misconstrued.[41] Science—practiced by a cadre of mainly male professionals—is under fire from political people (often women) demanding their due the same way men in general face pressure to give up their privileges. So, it's not just the average Joes out there who have been feeling squeezed economically, scientists themselves have felt the crunch and experience greater competition from fields associated with women. In 1989, when science studies scholar Haraway published her history of the field of primatology, identifying the many values and political visions that exemplified the field, a male scientist wrote an agitated review sporting the title "A Lab of One's Own," reappropriating the title of the famous feminist book by Virginia Woolf, *A Room of One's Own.*[42] It seems that scientists want to be left alone, free from the scrutiny of feminists.

HBE scholars fight not only about the nature of sex, but about professional status. Meanwhile, many of the feminist critics reproduce a central technique of showing disdain for patriarchal masculinity: nagging men into becoming more civil. Put another way, here are these guys being told to cool it—as dates, as lovers, as coworkers, as scientists. They are being told they're bogus bullies, while their jobs slip from their hairless palms. The war over scientific claims about male sexuality, then, is as much a war over men's status (e.g., as scientists and as workers) as it is a war over men's sexual nature. This points to our need to re-envision not only science but masculinity. It is with this alternative vision of manhood I wish to conclude the book.

A Great Leap Forward

I have argued that the caveman mystique is one manifestation of the shift from an industrial to a service economy and its accompanying culture of ornament. Social theorist Anthony Giddens tells us that in this postindustrial, posttraditional society, we increasingly try on and choose identities and lifestyles amidst a barrage of alternatives offered up by the capitalist marketplace for our consumption.[43] These choices are made in a consumer marketplace, with varying types of experts (whether scientific, spiritual, and/or political) all clamoring for men's devotion. As one such masculine identity available in that marketplace, the caveman limits men. With its assumptions of male–male competition and essentially different male and female natures, the caveman ethos prevents, if not actively resists, the democratization of intimacy, family, the workplace, and the social sphere.

The caveman mystique is empty, an image, just another affectation. It's a fiction that represents men's flight from fiction. In an era of the hyperreal, the quest for something unquestionably real is understandable. But the caveman isn't any more real than any other identity or affectation. Its scientific status satisfies a desperate search for authenticity, but the caveman identity is ultimately as artificial as the others. Susan Faludi elucidates the emptiness of ornamental masculinity, writing, "Conceiving of masculinity as something to be turns manliness into a detachable entity, at which point it instantly becomes ornamental, and about as innately 'masculine' as fake eyelashes are inherently 'feminine.'"[44] A caveman identity can fill the void in men's lives no better than new Tupperware could fill the void in the lives of 1950s women suffering the feminine mystique.

Barbara Ehrenreich argues that men some 40 to 50 years ago began to question the desirability of becoming providers to women and children.[45]

To stay free, they rejected the social obligation of working on behalf of a family and became playboys. Troublingly, some men rejected the confines of the breadwinner role *after* siring children, whom women were left tending with their lower-than-average incomes. In *Manhood in America*, Michael Kimmel refers to the strain, conflict, and alienation of the male role—felt as early as the 1960s, when the women's, civil rights, antiwar, and gay rights movements took off—as the "masculine mystique."[46] Few men could live up to the image of manhood as strong, silent, and successful. And even if they managed to do so, the role ended up riddled with restrictions, loneliness, and heart attacks.

When men consider their fantasized versions of themselves (the caveman being one such fantasy) against the reality of their life circumstances, they often find a palpable discrepancy. Many men feel powerless in their homes, at work, and in the global economy. They are not having, or even perhaps wanting, the sex they think their putatively insatiable libidos demand or enable. They are on Viagra or they are online trying to get dates or consuming pornography. The caveman offers an identity based on the identity men have lost (or think they have lost). Women have been gaining on men in the workplace and at home, and that slipping privilege is what gives an erotic charge to men's fantasized versions of their omnipotence.[47]

Kimmel notes that progressives in the 1960s and 1970s were hopeful that men would do something creative about their masculine malaise. And some surely did. Others wrote defensive responses to feminist demands that men stop their violence against women, share in household chores, and accept women as coworkers. For example, during the 1970s several reactionary books by men appeared, including George Gilder's *Sexual Suicide* and *Naked Nomads*, Steven Goldberg's *The Inevitability of Patriarchy*, and Norman Mailer's *The Prisoner of Sex*.[48] All of these books revealed resentment and resistance to feminist appeals for men to change. Gilder argued that men were biologically predisposed to aggression, competition, and violence, and that feminist change would create chaos, since women would no longer serve as a moral constraint on men's behavior.[49]

The caveman discourse emerged in this context of resistance to feminist changes and some men latched onto it. The caveman mystique is a response to the masculine mystique—but, while masquerading as a biological reality, it is a mystique nevertheless. However, both scientific claims about nature and about one definitive sexual script are losing authority. As Giddens notes, sexuality in posttraditional society has become increasingly "plastic," casting into question previously accepted assumptions that heterosexuality was the only natural, normal expression or identity.[50] We now live in an age characterized by pluralism—of lifestyles, of ideas, of identities. The gay rights movement has insisted on the legitimacy of sexual and family relationships beyond the Ozzie and Harriette norm. In this context, caveman sexuality cannot be anything more than one lifestyle choice among others. Hence, as a claim to authenticity, it is doomed to fail precisely because both the unchallengeable status of scientific claims about men's sexuality and the idea of one correct lifestyle are losing ground.

The caveman ethos reflects the penetration of personal identity by scientific discourse. Indeed, science serves us manhood wrapped in a tidy package of universal reason. It renders manhood and the heterosexuality associated with it unified, unchanging identity categories. Michel Foucault points out that sexuality became the property of individuals—an identity in and of itself—as sexual activity became separated from reproduction. Sexuality became a mode of social organization as the body and sex increased in importance. This occurred when the labor, fertility, and health of a large, mobile population became a major national concern.[51] Sexuality has since been a political battleground in the United States, and it garners special interest given the importance now placed on forging narratives of self, on lifestyle projects, and on intimacy. Giddens states that "sexuality is not the antithesis of a civilisation dedicated to economic growth and technical control, but the embodiment of its failure."[52] The rise of caveman sexuality, an identity available in the capitalist marketplace, only reveals the particular character of men's crisis.

The sexuality of the caveman is the quintessential episodic, genitally focused sexuality devoid of eroticism. Indeed, caveman sexuality is hardly a liberated one given its narrow focus on genital sexuality, high-intensity but low-emotion sex, sexual compulsiveness, an unacknowledged emotional dependence, and even overt rage and violence. Giddens calls this "episodic sexuality," which keeps men trapped in an antediluvian way of relating to women.[53]

Despite grounding the importance of their work in social change, evolutionary scientists work against social change surrounding gender precisely because, in our cultural context, biologizing identities turns those gender identities into new ethnicities.[54] Without understanding that identity works this way, HBE scholars tell men they are naturally predatory and heterosexual, and naturally different from women—and then leave us hanging on the hope that men can still change (or at least be decent). But the catch is, gender and sexual identities get treated as inner essences that are, like ethnicities, not only difficult but undesirable to change.[55] The recent Geico car insurance ads on television featuring a caveman who is offended by ads making him look stupid satirize this very formation of the caveman as an ethnicity. If gender is a new ethnicity, then supposed gender differences will be defended, not changed. As Kimmel puts it, such "sexual balkanization" imposes "a conceptual Iron Curtain inside our heads."[56]

Some research reveals that the more gender differentiated a society is, the more gendered violence it is likely to have.[57] Given this, the emphasis on sex-based biological brain differences, whether or not it is scientifically accurate, can lead men to think of themselves as sharply different from women and to act different from them in a variety of ways HBE scholars never predicted. Indeed, we have good reason to see men's behavior as the result of stories about, rather than as simple evidence of, human male nature.

Kimmel argues that the quest to prove manhood, a pastime of the American male for 200 years, is "a battle that can never be won."[58] Such efforts

> lead men on the historical and quixotic quest to demonstrate what can never be successfully, finally, demonstrated, to strive to achieve what can never be achieved. The trail blazed by the Self-Made Man is a spiral path leading only back to itself, to a relentless retesting of an unprovable ambition.[59]

Identity is better understood as a reflexively organized project, not some authentic essence. Giddens suggests that men need to be able to "construct a narrative of self that allows them to come to terms with an increasingly democratised and reordered sphere of personal life."[60] The caveman mystique's hollow narrative of self keeps men from embracing (or even comprehending) the more democratized, reordered sphere they struggle in.

Kimmel argues that the male liberation movement of the 1970s fought the masculine mystique unsuccessfully because it simply encouraged men to change the roles they played. Without transforming the economic and social structures that put men into the traditional male role, the male liberation movement "would easily sour into the whine of a new voice of victimhood."[61] Those who weren't whining in New Agey men's movements were resentful. Teenagers celebrating rock or country singers whose bitterness at immigrants, queers, and women (groups who presumably hold all the power over middle-class white men) reveal that American men are angry and taking it out on those with less power.[62]

Certainly other men embrace feelings of pride when they act in caring and compassionate ways (as in Jeff Hood's *Silverback Gorilla* treatise, discussed in chapter 3). But this attitude does not go far enough because it neglects to question the status of science, identity, or gender. Instead, social issues are presented as issues of personality and individual pathology. Tame your inner gorilla—and live as an enlightened caveman.[63] If men use evolutionary narratives to understand their inner drives and desires, they may or may not control those putatively innate drives. But even if they do, they only tone down a male-dominant society.

Following W. Bradford Wilcox's 2004 book, *Soft Patriarchs, New Men*, I call this kind of manhood *soft patriarchy*.[64] The Promise Keepers—a movement of over a million Christian American men that gained momentum in the 1990s—push men to renew a promise they made under God to be kind heads of household, and to rule over women and children with a good-natured, respectful mission. This does not ever put men and women on equal footing. They recruit men to be better husbands and fathers—what seems like a progressive way to increase gender justice and men's involvement with their families—without ever challenging men's sense that they are kings of their homes and families. The Promise Keepers encourage women to accept this "patriarchal bargain" in order to get some commitment from men to their families.[65] The logic of soft patriarchy allows men to continue to demand a position of power in relationship to women, whether that relationship is sexual, working, or familial.

As I have shown, men's power and authority have been under fire. With the world caving in on men this way, it's no wonder they're "going caveman." Both the outright anger at those who are gaining on men and the soft patriarchy of the compassionate gorillas who consider themselves innately aggressive yet willing to reign it in employ a caveman mystique in response to a masculine crisis and its concomitant social upheaval. But embracing the Stone Age will not stave off the postmodern age.

Men must stop prostrating themselves to science. They must question their desire for the kind of authenticity a scientific account of their nature presumably provides. Even if men want to look for an identity in scientific claims about male nature, they have to recognize that such claims will change. Science is not a stable discipline. The imperatives of scientific expertise, to which the moral future of humanity, under this logic, must be subjected, only anchors our possibilities of an enlightened future to the EEA. In the realm of sexual mores, this scientism ultimately promotes a system that is substantively, even if not formally, patriarchal.

Men need not concede to caveman claims. And by this I do not mean that men can rebel against their sexist genes. Men do not need to swallow whole the evolutionary explanation that their genes are controlling them unless they rebel against them. There is enough doubt about these claims, and insufficient reasons (in terms of policy and "social engineering") to heed them. Besides, there's a better narrative of manhood out there; a better narrative of our bodies and their relationship to culture; a better way to understand science; a better understanding of science and popular culture; and a better way to appreciate the relationship between science and politics.

I'm suggesting that men can cast off the burden of the caveman mystique. Kimmel argues that men cannot just change their role and how they perceive it, but instead must join others struggling for social justice. He calls this a "democratic manhood" in which men stand up against injustice both in their personal lives and in the larger society. Giddens' work on the politics of lifestyle choices suggests that when people demand that society make room for their lifestyle choice, they are also, in the end, engaging in social change because they must also demand new laws, policies, and other institutional changes that accommodate their lifestyles. For instance, men who want to take a bigger role in their children's lives must demand better family leave policies and family-friendly work schedules—for men as well as for women.

If the male revolt against "breadwinnerdom" in part stemmed from the way in which fitting into a role felt constricting, the caveman ethos may feel equally constricting. The caveman mystique robs men of the rewards of the democratization of personal life. As the feminine mystique crushed women's spirits by keeping them dependent on men, so the caveman mystique crushes men's potential by defining them as moral and physical drifters, who supposedly find fulfillment in chance encounters. The caveman mystique keeps men from the rewards of moral accountability, shared respect, shared resources, family ties, and commitment (including a commitment to future generations). To break out of the cave, men must stop allowing evolutionary theory to drive their self-definitions.

They must question the authority of science and use their imaginations to create a new masculinity, including a new sexual manner.

Men can embrace a relational sexuality rather than an episodic one. Episodic sexuality encourages a flight from intimacy and the connections that link sexuality, self-identity, and intimacy.[66] Sexuality is now plastic—and so monogamy is now about trust, not about a patriarchal double standard to which heterosexual couples are held in state-certified marriages. Men can overcome that "lapsed emotional narrative of self" and love women or men as equals, in an intimate way, and care for those with less power (their children or aging parents, for example).[67]

Darwinian thought moved sex away from sin in the cultural imagination, but not all sexual behaviors (rape and pedophilia, for example) are morally acceptable. Social regulation of sexuality must occur if we are to live in a free society in which one person doesn't trample on the civil liberties of another. We are forced to make complicated political arguments about sex and its regulation. And these arguments, as I hope I have shown, are inescapably political. Science cannot, therefore, tell us what is morally acceptable sexual behavior, and it certainly cannot justify any particular behavior. The caveman defense of date rape is satirized on a T-shirt for sale on the cafepress.com Web site, which features user-created merchandise. The T-shirt reminds men that not raping is as elementary as getting verbal consent by depicting a caveman in a fur pelt holding a club along with the saying: "DATING 101: ASK FIRST." Even a caveman should be able to understand the difference between consent and coercion, and so the T-shirt positions men's use of the caveman narrative as a flimsy excuse for immoral behavior.

I believe that questioning the link between science and morality while simultaneously insisting upon gendered subjectivity as textual rather than biological, animal, or essential would have made the New York City group sexual assaults in 2000 that much harder for individual men to rationalize and therefore carry out. It would make them harder for our society to accept for the same reason. I hope that by deconstructing the naturalized, taken-for-granted beliefs about men's sexuality, both men and women might expand their physical, erotic, creative, and moral potential and relate more critically to scientific claims about people. Indeed we have good reasons to deconstruct, rather than defend, the caveman.

Science cannot save men, and it cannot resolve political problems between the sexes. Men can and should rise above bad behaviors and

Dating 101.

treat women with respect. But they do not need to believe in a biololgical
original sin in order to do this. So instead of taming men, I'm suggesting
we think about knowledge and identities as wild.[68] Instead of universal,
grand, and all-encompassing theories of male nature, we can emphasize
local realities. We can embrace the diversity of masculinities and the ways
in which men and women can be similar to one another as well as different. Steven Seidman urges us to consider identity open and contestable,
which "encourages the public surfacing of differences or a culture where
multiple voices and interests are heard."[69]

   In chapter 3, I suggested that too many men unreflexively live out and
quite literally carry around, through their bodily comportment, the ideology of the caveman mystique. However, men are not bound and determined by cultural or economic forces. Men can create a new habitus and
with it alter the social conditions that gave rise to the caveman mystique.

In other words, men can use their bodies to rebel against the dominant caveman discourse. A Foucauldian strategy of disidentification recognizes that identities are important sites of historical and cultural forces, not natural expressions.[70] A strategy of disidentification allows men to take some responsibility for their sexual choices and makes room for men to change their relationship to their bodies, to scientific discourse, and to the whole concept of manhood.

Men must use their imaginations—not the authority of science—to create a new masculinity, for without imagination there can be no new consciousness. I hope that by gaining a broader, sociological view of themselves as gendered beings in a gendered society, men might see the caveman identity as an empty fiction. I've explained the appeal of the scientific narrative about men emerging because of our culture's faith in science as a neutral arbiter of political disputes. I've shown that arguments over men's sexual nature are as much arguments about the authority of science and men's status (as scientists and as workers). In so doing, I suggest that our knowledge of knowledge itself evolve. I also insist that our knowledge of identity evolve. Manhood itself must morph into something new.

Men can take a great leap forward and become new kinds of men. I call this new manhood *Homo textual*. This new man understands identity as socially constructed and consequential.[71] *Homo textual* understands his manhood not through the grand narrative of science, but as a production of texts—scientific, legal, and political. *Homo textual* has what social theorist Patricia Clough called, in another context, a "politicized self-consciousness about textuality."[72] *Homo textual* establishes relationships beyond preestablished identities. *Homo textual* might have specific sexual preferences, but understands such preferences as fluid aspects of biography, culture, and history—in addition to biology. *Homo textual* has a body—but not a body bearing the meaning of a story assumed to be objective. *Homo textual* is a critical author of meaning. *Homo textual* tells new stories with his body. And as such, *Homo textual* is a sexy leap in a new direction.

NOTES

Introduction

1. I am appropriating Robin Baker's term *sperm wars* from his book *Sperm Wars: Infidelity, Sexual Conflict, and Other Bedroom Battles* (New York: Thunder's Mouth, 2006). I do not wish to imply, however, that Baker would use the concept in this exact same way. By "sperm war" Baker means something more precise than simply the general idea that men were in competition with one another for access to women. He describes sperm warfare, in which men have different types of sperm: egg getters and kamikaze sperm that prevent the sperm of other males from reaching the egg. This, of course, implies that the different types of sperm evolved to solve the adaptive problem of sperm competition, which implies that ancestral women mated with more than one man in the space of a week often enough for males with destroyer sperm to have better reproductive success.
2. Robert Wright, "Our Cheating Hearts," *Time*, August 15, 1994, 44–52. By "popular" I mean general, widespread, and frequent. I also intend to make a distinction between the professional and the popular. For a discussion of tensions in the usage of "popular" (as in "popular culture" and "popular speech"), see Pierre Bourdieu, "Did You Say 'Popular'?" in *Language and Symbolic Power*, ed. and intro. John B. Thompson, trans. Gino Raymond and Matthew Adamson (Cambridge, MA: Harvard University Press, 1991), 90–104.
3. Mary Ellen Strote, "Man the Visual Animal," *Muscle and Fitness*, February 1994, 166.
4. See Betty Friedan, *The Feminine Mystique* (New York: Dell, 1963).
5. Laurence Gonzales, "The Biology of Attraction," *Men's Health* 20, no. 7 (2005): 186–93.
6. Ibid., 192.
7. Ibid., 193.
8. Amy Alkon, "Many Men Fantasize during Sex, But It Isn't a Talking Point," *Winston-Salem Journal*, September 29, 2005, 34.
9. Steven E. Rhoads, *Taking Sex Differences Seriously* (San Francisco: Encounter Books, 2004), 4.

10. For defenses of the study of the popularization of scientific discourse, and exemplary studies of the popularization of Darwinian discourse in different eras, see Alfred Kelly, *The Descent of Darwin: The Popularization of Darwinism in Germany, 1860–1914* (Chapel Hill: University of North Carolina Press, 1981); and Alvar Ellegård, *Darwin and the General Reader: The Reception of Darwin's Theory of Evolution in the British Press, 1859–1872* (Chicago: University of Chicago Press, 1990).

11. Evolutionary biology provides the conceptual framework within which psychological, evolutionary, and genetic developments are logically integrated. According to Edward O. Wilson in *Consilience: The Unity of Knowledge* (New York: Vintage, 1998), 163, sociobiology is "the systematic study of the biological basis of social behavior in all kinds of organisms, including humans." Evolutionary psychology is defined in David Buss, *Evolutionary Psychology: The New Science of the Mind* (Needham Heights, MA: Allyn and Bacon, 1999), 34, as "a new scientific synthesis of modern evolutionary biology and psychology."

12. See Mary Maxwell, ed., *The Sociobiological Imagination* (Albany: State University of New York Press, 1991).

13. The European version is the European Sociobiological Society. The European Sociobiological Society, which began in 1981 as the European Sociobiology Study Group, voted in 2000 to merge with the International Society for Human Ethology (ISHE).

14. See Kelly, *The Descent of Darwin*, 6–7, for this very argument in the context of his own study of popularization.

15. Michel Foucault, *The History of Sexuality, Volume. 1: An Introduction* (New York: Random House, 1978).

16. Judith Butler, *Bodies that Matter: On the Discursive Limits of Sex* (New York: Routledge, 1993), 10.

17. See Roland Barthes, *Mythologies*, trans. Annette Lavers (New York: Hill and Wang, 1972).

18. See Sarah Blaffer Hrdy, *Mother Nature: Maternal Instincts and How They Shape the Human Species* (New York: Ballantine, 2000).

19. See Marlene Zuk, *Sexual Selections: What We Can and Can't Learn about Sex from Animals* (Berkeley and Los Angeles: University of California Press, 2002).

20. See Elisabeth A. Lloyd, *The Case of the Female Orgasm: Bias in the Science of Evolution* (Cambridge, MA: Harvard University Press, 2005).

21. See Ullica Segerstråle, *Defenders of the Truth: The Battle for Science in the Sociobiology Debate and Beyond* (Oxford: Oxford University Press, 2000).

22. See Steve Fuller, *The New Sociological Imagination* (London: Sage, 2006) for a discussion of the history of sociology and the significance of a biological challenge to social science.

23. Susan Bordo, *The Male Body: A New Look at Men in Public and Private* (New York: Farrar, Strauss, and Giroux, 1999); Susan Faludi, *Stiffed: The Betrayal of the American Man* (New York: HarperCollins, 1999); Michael Kimmel, *Manhood in America: A Cultural History* (New York: Free Press, 1997).

24. See Maurice Berger, Brian Wallis, and Simon Watson, eds. *Constructing Masculinity* (New York: Routledge, 1995).

25. Mark Erickson, *Science, Culture and Society* (Cambridge U.K.: Polity Press, 2005), 224.

26. Martha McCaughey, *Real Knockouts: The Physical Feminism of Women's Self-Defense* (New York: New York University Press, 1997).

27. See Dorothy Nelkin and M. Susan Lindee, *DNA Mystique: The Gene As a Cultural Icon* (New York: W. H. Freeman, 1995).

28. John Fiske, *Television Culture* (New York: Methuen, 1987), 1.

29. See John Fiske, "Intertextuality," in *Popular Culture: Production and Consumption*, eds. C. Lee Harrington and Denise D. Bielby (Malden, MA: Blackwell, 2000), 219–33.

30. Fiske, *Television Culture*, 4.
31. See Steven Seidman, *Contested Knowledge: Social Theory in the Postmodern Era* (Malden, MA: Blackwell, 1994).
32. See E. O. Wilson, *On Human Nature* (Cambridge, MA: Harvard University Press, 1978); and Richard Dawkins, *The Selfish Gene* (Oxford, U.K.: Oxford University Press, 1976).
33. See E. O. Wilson, *Consilience* (New York: Knopf, 1998); and E. O. Wilson, "The Biological Basis of Morality," *Atlantic Monthly*, April (1998).
34. See Robin Baker, *Sperm Wars*; R. Robin Baker and Mark A. Bellis, *Human Sperm Competition: Copulation, Masturbation, and Infidelity* (London: Chapman and Hall, 1994).
35. Clive Bromhall, dir., "Beyond Survival" (episode) in *Desmond Morris' The Human Animal: A Personal View of the Human Species*. New York: Discovery Communications, 1999.
36. Kelly, *The Descent of Darwin*, 4.
37. Nelkin and Lindee, *The DNA Mystique*, 11–13.
38. See Graham Allen, *Intertextuality: The New Critical Idiom* (New York: Routledge, 2000).
39. Barbara Ehrenreich deserves credit for first adding the "on foreplay" to the usual wording. See Ehrenereich, "How 'Natural' Is Rape?" *Time*, January 31, 2000, 88.
40. See Judith Butler, *Gender Trouble: Feminism and the Subversion of Identity* (New York: Routledge, 1990).
41. Ann Arbor Science for the People Editorial Collective, *Biology as a Social Weapon* (Ann Arbor, MI: Burgess, 1977), quoted in Peter Singer, "Ethics and Sociobiology," *Zygon* 19, no. 2 (1984): 153.
42. See Devendra Singh, "Adaptive Significance of Female Physical Attractiveness: Role of Waist-to-Hip Ratio," *Journal of Personality and Social Psychology* 65 (1993): 293–307.
43. This is W. Bradford Wilcox's term. See Wilcox, *Soft Patriarchs, New Men: How Christianity Shapes Fathers and Husbands* (Chicago: University of Chicago Press, 2004), which I discuss further in chapter 5.
44. Susan Faludi, *Stiffed: The Betrayal of the American Man* (New York: HarperCollins, 1999), 45.
45. Steven Seidman, *Difference Troubles: Queering Social Theory and Sexual Politics* (Cambridge: Cambridge, U.K. University Press, 1997), 93.

Chapter 1

1. See, for example, Abigail Solomon-Godeau, "Male Trouble," in *Constructing Masculinity*, ed. Maurice Berger, Brian Wallis, and Simon Watson (New York: Routledge, 1995), 69–76.
2. Susan Faludi, *Stiffed: The Betrayal of the American Man* (New York: HarperCollins, 1999).
3. Irene Padavic and Barbara Reskin, *Women and Men at Work*, 2nd ed. (Thousand Oaks, CA: Pine Forge, 2002).
4. Carmen DeNavas-Walt, Bernadette D. Proctor, and Cheryl Hill Lee, "Income, Poverty, and Health Insurance Coverage in the United States: 2005," in *U.S. Census Bureau, Current Population Reports* (Washington, D.C.: U.S. Government Printing Office, 2006), 60–231.
5. Paul Ryscavage, *Gender-Related Shifts in the Distribution of Wages, 1994*. Accessed May 2, 2003 from http://www.bls.gov/opub/mlr/1994/07/art1full.pdf.
6. Faludi, *Stiffed*.
7. Ibid., 38.
8. Ibid., 40.
9. Ibid., 38.

10. See Michael S. Kimmel, *The Gender of Desire: Essays on Male Sexuality* (Albany: State University of New York Press, 2005), 227–34, for a similar argument about ethnic nationalist violence. Kimmel argues that such violence is a gendered protest by frustrated lower middle-class young men who feel cheated out of the economic rewards they expected, but will not likely get, as they become incorporated into the global economy. These men's violence expresses a frustrated sense of entitlement to experience the working life, control, and power they were raised to expect to have as men.

11. Barbara Ehrenreich, "The Decline of Patriarchy," in *Constructing Masculinity*, eds. Maurice Berger, Brian Wallis, and Simon Watson (New York: Routledge, 1995), 284–90.

12. Of course, it should be noted that even in households in which a woman earns the same amount or more than her male partner, the man often still dominates.

13. See Padavic and Reskin, *Women and Men at Work*, 129.

14. Ehrenreich, "Decline."

15. Barbara Ehrenreich, *The Hearts of Men: American Dreams and the Flight From Commitment* (Garden City, NY: Anchor Books, 1983), 169.

16. Neal King, *Heroes in Hard Times: Cop Action Movies in the U.S.* (Philadelphia: Temple University Press, 1999), 6–8.

17. Faludi, *Stiffed*, 31.

18. Ibid., 31.

19. Ibid., 45.

20. Ehrenreich, *Hearts*, 145–47.

21. Desmond Morris, *The Naked Ape: A Zoologist's Study of the Human Animal* (1967; reprint New York: Dell, 1999).

22. See David M. Buss, "Sex Differences in Human Mate Preferences: Evolutionary Hypotheses Tested in 37 Cultures," *Behavioral and Brain Sciences* 12 (1989): 1–49; David M. Buss, et al., "International Preferences in Selecting Mates: A Study of 37 Cultures," *Journal of Cross-Cultural Psychology* 21 (1990):5–47; and David M. Buss, *The Evolution of Desire: Strategies of Human Mating* (New York: Basic Books, 1994).

23. See Buss, *The Evolution of Desire*.

24. See Martin Daly and Margo Wilson, *Sex, Evolution, and Behavior* (Boston: Willard Grant, 1983).

25. Ibid., 6; emphasis in the original.

26. See Donald Symons, *The Evolution of Human Sexuality* (New York: Oxford University Press, 1979).

27. See Edward O. Wilson, *On Human Nature* (Cambridge, MA: Harvard University Press, 1987).

28. Ibid., 196.

29. See Buss, *The Evolution of Desire*; Daly and Wilson, *Sex, Evolution, and Behavior*; Symons, *Evolution*; and Wilson, *On Human Nature*.

30. See Judith Butler, *Gender Trouble: Feminism and the Subversion of Identity* (New York: Routledge, 1990); Bernice L. Hausman, "Sex Before Gender: Charlotte Perkins Gilman and the Evolutionary Paradigm of Utopia," *Feminist Studies* 24, no. 3 (1998): 488–510; and Randy Thornhill and Craig T. Palmer, *A Natural History of Rape: Biological Bases of Sexual Coercion* (Cambridge, MA: MIT Press, 2000), 198.

31. David Barash, *The Whisperings Within: Evolution and the Origin of Human Nature* (New York: Harper and Row, 1979), 31.

32. See Catherine Salmon and Donald Symons, *Warrior Lovers: Erotic Fiction, Evolution and Female Sexuality* (New Haven, CT: Yale University Press, 2003).

33. See Michael W. Wiederman and Erica Kendall, "Evolution, Sex, and Jealousy: Investigation with a Sample from Sweden," *Evolution and Human Behavior* 20, no. 2 (1999): 121–28.

34. Ibid.

35. Margo Wilson and Martin Daly, "The Man Who Mistook His Wife for a Chattel," in *The Adapted Mind: Evolutionary Psychology and the Generation of Culture*, eds. Jermone H. Barkow, Leda Cosmides and John Tooby (New York: Oxford University Press, 1992), 300.

36. Thornhill and Palmer, *A Natural History of Rape*, 143.

37. Ibid., 144.

38. Susan Brownmiller, *Against Our Will: Men, Women, and Rape* (New York: Ballantine, 1975).

39. Thornhill and Palmer, *A Natural History of Rape*, 144.

40. For a specific history, see Lisa Duggan and Nan D. Hunter, *Sex Wars: Sexual Dissent and Political Culture* (New York: Routledge, 1995).

41. I want to be clear that *I myself* am not suggesting MacKinnon and Dworkin's work is "antimale."

42. Feminist evolutionary theorists are the exception here, of course.

43. Naomi Weisstein, letter to the editor, *New York Times Book Review*, April 23, 2000, 4.

44. David M. Buss and Neil M. Malamuth, "Introduction," in *Sex, Power, Conflict: Evolutionary and Feminist Perspectives*, eds. David M. Buss and Neil Malamuth (New York: Oxford University Press, 1996), 3; emphasis in the original.

45. See Paul R. Gross and Norman Leavitt, *Higher Superstition: The Academic Left and Its Quarrels with Science* (Baltimore: John Hopkins University Press, 1994).

46. See Alan D. Sokal, "Transgressing the Boundaries: Toward a Transformative Hermeneutics of Quantum Gravity," *Social Text* 46–47 (1996): 217–52.

47. Alan D. Sokal, "A Physicist Experiments with Cultural Studies," *Lingua Franca* 6, no. 4 (1996): 62–64.

48. I'll leave aside here the fact—which seemed unbeknownst to Sokal and his cheerleaders—that *Social Text* is not a peer-reviewed journal, but is published instead by an editorial collective. As such, outside reviewers are not used; the members of the collective decide whether or not to publish any given submission.

49. See Thomas F. Gieryn, *Cultural Boundaries of Science: Credibility on the Line* (Chicago: The University of Chicago Press, 1999), 336–62, for an excellent and succinct history of the science wars.

50. Gross and Leavitt, *Higher Superstition*, 12, 47, 50, 52, 55, 81.

51. Alan D. Sokal, "What the Social Text Affair Does and Does Not Prove: A Critical Look at 'Science Studies,'" in *After the Science Wars*, eds. Keith M. Ashman and Philip S. Baringer (New York: Routledge, 2001), 15–16.

52. See, for example, Meika Loe, *The Rise of Viagra: How the Little Blue Pill Changed Sex in America* (New York: New York University Press, 2004).

53. Sokal, "A Physicist Experiments," 62.

54. In case any readers are wondering what it is social constructionists do say about gravity, they simply point out that the "law of gravity" is a concept humans created to describe this phenomenon, and that the law itself doesn't cause a body to fall; see John Michael, *Anxious Intellects: Academic Professionals, Public Intellectuals, and Enlightenment Values* (Durham, NC: Duke University Press, 2000).

55. Steve Fuller, "Science Studies through the Looking Glass: An Intellectual Itinerary," in *Beyond the Science Wars: The Missing Discourse About Science and Society*, ed. Ullica Segerstrâle (Albany: State University of New York Press, 2000), 204.

56. See *Evolution, Gender, and Rape*, ed. Cheryl B. Travis (Cambridge: MIT Press, 2003).

57. Gieryn, *Cultural Boundaries of Science*, 3.

58. Diana Scully, *Understanding Sexual Violence: A Study of Convicted Rapists* (Boston: Unwin Hyman, 1990).

59. Thornhill and Palmer, *A Natural History of Rape*, 128.

60. Peggy Reeves Sanday, Fraternity Gang Rape: Sex, Brotherhood, and Privilege on Campus (New York: New York University Press, 1990), quoted in Thornhill and Palmer, *A Natural History of Rape*, 147.
61. See, for example, Andrea Dworkin, *Intercourse* (New York: Free Press, 1987); Catharine A. MacKinnon, *Toward a Feminist Theory of the State* (Cambridge, MA: Harvard University Press, 1989); and John Stoltenberg, *Refusing to Be a Man: Essays on Sex and Justice* (Portland, OR: Breitenbush, 1989).
62. Timothy Beneke, *Rape: What They Have to Say About Sexual Violence* (New York: St. Martin's Press, 1983), quoted in Thornhill and Palmer, *A Natural History of Rape*, 147.
63. See Anthony Giddens, *Transformation of Intimacy: Sexuality, Love and Eroticism in Modern Societies* (Stanford, CA: Stanford University Press, 1992).
64. See Stoltenberg, *Refusing to Be a Man*.
65. Steven Seidman, *Contested Knowledge: Social Theory in the Postmodern Era* (Malden, MA: Blackwell, 1994).

Chapter 2

1. See Brian Easlea, *Science and Sexual Oppression: Patriarchy's Confrontation with Woman and Nature* (London: Weidenfeld and Nicolson, 1981).
2. See Easlea, *Science and Sexual Oppression*; and R.M. Young, *Darwin's Metaphor: Nature's Place in Victorian Culture* (New York: Cambridge University Press, 1985).
3. Stephen Jay Gould, *Wonderful Life: The Burgess Shale and the Nature of History* (New York: W. W. Norton, 1989), 290.
4. See George C. Williams, "Huxley's Evolution and Ethics in Sociobiological Perspective," *Zygon* 23, no. 4 (1988): 383–407.
5. Alfred Kelly, *The Descent of Darwin: The Popularization of Darwinism in Germany, 1860–1914* (Chapel Hill: University of North Carolina Press, 1981), 144.
6. Alvar Ellegård, *Darwin and the General Reader: The Reception of Darwin's Theory of Evolution in the British Press, 1859–1872* (Chicago: University of Chicago Press, 1990), 99.
7. Kelly, *The Descent of Darwin*, 77–78.
8. See James Thompson Bixby, *The Crisis in Morals* (Boston: Roberts Brothers, 1891).
9. Asa Gray, "Design versus Necessity: Discussion between Two Readers of Darwin's Treatise on the Origin of Species, upon Its Natural Theology," *American Journal of Science and Arts* 30 (1860): 226–39, quoted in Robert M. Young, "The Meanings of Darwinism: Then and Now," *Science as Culture* 11, no. 1 (2001): 107.
10. Charles Darwin to Joseph Dalton Hooker, 1856, quoted in Easlea, *Science and Sexual Oppression*, 105.
11. T.H. Huxley, "Agnosticism," *Nineteenth Century* 24 (1889): 191, quoted in Misia Landau, "Human Evolution as Narrative," *American Scientist* 72 (1984): 265.
12. See Young, *Darwin's Metaphor*.
13. See Robert J. Richards, *Darwin and the Emergence of Evolutionary Theories of Mind and Behavior* (Chicago: University of Chicago Press, 1987).
14. Adam Sedgwick to Charles Darwin, Nov. 24, 1859, quoted in Easlea, *Science and Sexual Oppression*, 110.
15. Ellegård, *Darwin and the General Reader*, 301–2.
16. Richards, *Darwin and the Emergence of Evolutionary Theories*, 188–89.
17. Herbert Spencer, *The Principles of Ethics* (New York: D. Appleton, 1897), quoted in William S. Quillian, Jr., *The Moral Theory of Evolutionary Naturalism* (New Haven, CT: Yale University Press, 1945), 17.
18. C.M. Williams, *Review of the Systems of Ethics Founded on Evolution* (New York: Macmillan, 1893), quoted in Quillian, *The Moral Theory*, 17.
19. Michael Ruse, "Evolutionary Ethics: A Phoenix Arisen," *Zygon* 21, no. 1 (1986): 95–96.

20. Arthur Keith, The *Religion of a Darwinist* (London: Watts, 1925), quoted in Raymond B. Cattell, *Beyondism: Religion from Science* (New York: Praeger, 1987), 143.
21. Cattell, *Beyondism*, 77.
22. Keith, *The Religion of a Darwinist*, quoted in Cattell, *Beyondism*, 71–72.
23. Charles Darwin, *The Descent of Man, and Selection in Relation to Sex* (London: John Murray, 1871) quoted in Landau, "Human Evolution," 265.
24. Bixby, *The Crisis in Morals*, v, viii.
25. Kelly, *The Descent of Darwin*, 100.
26. Ibid., 100.
27. Dorothy Nelkin and M. Susan Lindee, *The DNA Mystique: The Gene As a Cultural Icon* (New York: W. H. Freeman, 1995).
28. Richards, *Darwin and the Emergence of Evolutionary Theories*, 536.
29. George C. Williams, *Adaptation and Natural Selection* (Princeton, NJ: Princeton University Press, 1966).
30. See Williams, "Huxley's Evolution."
31. Ibid., 399.
32. Philip Hefner, "Sociobiology, Ethics, and Theology," *Zygon* 19, no. 2 (1984): 201.
33. Edward O. Wilson, *On Human Nature* (Cambridge, MA: Harvard University Press, 1978), 201.
34. Ruse, "Evolutionary Ethics," 95.
35. Robert Wright, *Three Scientists and Their Gods: Looking for Meaning in an Age of Information* (New York: Times Books, 1988).
36. Ralph Burhoe, "War, Peace, and Religion's Biocultural Evolution," *Zygon* 21, no. 4 (1986): 460.
37. Will Durant, *The Story of Philosophy* (New York: Simon and Schuster, 1934), quoted in Eric J. Chaisson, "Our Cosmic Heritage," *Zygon* 23, no. 4 (1988): 476.
38. William A. Rottschaefer, review of *Science and Moral Priority: Merging Mind, Brain, and Human Values*, by Roger W. Sperry, *Zygon* 19, no. 2 (1984): 244.
39. Wilson, *On Human Nature*, 196.
40. David Martinsen and William A. Rottschaefer, "Singer, Sociobiology, and Values: Pure Reason Versus Empirical Reason," *Zygon* 19, no. 2 (1984): 159.
41. Ibid.
42. Rottschaefer, review, 246.
43. Williams, "Huxley's Evolution," 402–3.
44. David Barash, *The Whisperings Within: Evolution and the Origin of Human Nature* (New York: Harper and Row, 1979), 21, quoted in Donna J. Haraway, "In the Beginning Was the Word: The Genesis of Biological Theory," *Signs* 6, no. 3 (1981): 471.
45. Richard Dawkins, *The Selfish Gene* (Oxford, U.K.: Oxford University Press, 1976), 36.
46. Ibid., 215.
47. Joseph Lopreato, "Toward a Theory of Genuine Altruism in *Homo Sapiens*," *Ethology and Sociobiology* 2 (1981): 124, quoted in Williams, "Huxley's Evolution," 403.
48. Williams, "Huxley's Evolution," 403.
49. David M. Buss, *The Evolution of Desire: Strategies of Human Mating.* (New York: Basic Books, 1994), 5.
50. Jared Diamond, "Preface," in *Why Is Sex Fun? The Evolution of Human Sexuality* (New York: Basic Books, 1997), x.
51. Richard D. Alexander, *Darwinism and Human Affairs* (Seattle: University of Washington Press, 1979), 277.
52. See Randy Thornhill and Craig T. Palmer, *A Natural History of Rape: Biological Bases of Sexual Coercion* (Cambridge, MA: MIT Press, 2000).
53. Hefner, "Sociobiology, Ethics, and Theology," 205–6.
54. Alexander, *Darwinism and Human Affairs*, xvi.

55. Bobbi S. Low, *Why Sex Matters: A Darwinian Look at Human Behavior* (Princeton, NJ: Princeton University Press, 2000), 258.
56. Alexander, *Darwinism and Human Affairs*, xiv.
57. See John Tooby and Leda Cosmides, *The Adapted Mind: Evolutionary Psychology and the Generation of Culture* (Oxford, U.K.: Oxford University Press, 1992); and Edward O. Wilson, *Consilience: The Unity of Knowledge* (New York: Vintage, 1998).
58. Robert Wright, *The Moral Animal: Evolutionary Psychology and Everyday Life* (New York: Pantheon, 1994).
59. Ibid., 130.
60. Ibid., 137.
61. John H. Beckstrom, *Darwinism Applied: Evolutionary Paths to Social Goals* (Westport, CT: Praeger, 1993), 2.
62. Ibid., 5.
63. Ibid., 23.
64. Ibid., 56.
65. Ibid., 59.
66. Ibid., 2.
67. Daniel C. Dennett, *Darwin's Dangerous Idea: Evolution and the Meanings of Life* (New York: Simon & Schuster, 1995), 23.
68. Ibid., 21; emphasis in the original.
69. See Anthony Giddens, *The Transformation of Intimacy: Sexuality, Love and Eroticism in Modern Societies* (Stanford, CA: Stanford University Press, 1992).
70. John Michael, *Anxious Intellects: Academic Professionals, Public Intellectuals, and Enlightenment Values* (Durham, NC: Duke University Press, 2000), 131.
71. There is a tension in the HBE field between those scientists with what Steve Fuller, "The Reenchantment of Science: A Fit End to the Science Wars?" in *After the Science Wars*, eds. Keith M. Ashman and Philip S. Baringer (New York: Routledge, 2001), 183–208, calls a "puritanical" understanding of science (that science should be kept separate from social concerns) and those who see themselves as not only able but obliged to contribute to political discussions related to their research to use science to reform society. Hence, some evolutionary scholars got upset with the authors of *A Natural History of Rape* for including a discussion on rape prevention in their book. Those scholars saw the book as mixing science and politics inappropriately.
72. Mary Hawkesworth, "Feminist Epistemology: A Survey of the Field," *Women and Politics* 7, no. 3 (1987): 118.
73. Steven Seidman, *Difference Troubles: Queering Social Theory and Sexual Politics* (Cambridge, MA: Cambridge University Press, 1997), 206.
74. See Susan Bordo, *The Male Body* (New York: Farrar, Strauss, and Giroux, 1999); and Michael S. Kimmel, *Manhood in America: A Cultural History* (New York: Free Press, 1996).
75. Fuller, "The Reenchantment of Science."
76. See Bernice L. Hausman, *Mother's Milk: Breastfeeding Controversies in American Culture* (New York: Routledge, 2003) for an analysis of "stone age mothering" in the context of debates over breast- versus bottle feeding.

Chapter 3

1. Dorothy Nelkin and M. Susan Lindee, *The DNA Mystique: The Gene As a Cultural Icon* (New York: W. H. Freeman and Company, 1995), 11.
2. Ibid., 79–80.
3. Sylvia Cary, "The Isolation Principle," *Men's Fitness*, October 1993, 67.
4. Ibid..
5. Robert Bly, interview on PBS television show "No Safe Place: Violence Against Women" (March 27, 1998).

6. Robert Bly, *Iron John: A Book About Men* (Reading, MA: Addison-Wesley, 1990), 38.
7. John Gray, *Men Are from Mars, Women Are from Venus: The Classic Guide to Understanding the Opposite Sex* (New York: HarperCollins, 2002).
8. Warren Farrell, *Why Men Are the Way They Are* (New York: McGraw-Hill, 1986).
9. Jean-Jacques Annaud, dir., *Quest for Fire* (Paris: Belstar, 1981; DVD release, Los Angeles: Fox Home Entertainment, 2003).
10. Smith and Doe, *What Men Don't Want Women to Know: The Secrets, the Lies, the Unspoken Truth* (New York: St. Martin's, 1998).
11. Ibid., 53.
12. Ibid., 68–69.
13. Ibid., 11; 16.
14. Ibid., 93.
15. See Randy Thornhill and Craig T. Palmer, *A Natural History of Rape: Biological Bases of Sexual Coercion* (Cambridge, MA: MIT Press, 2000).
16. Jennifer Pozner, "In Rape Debate, Controversy Trumps Credibility: 'Natural' Sexual Assualt Theory 'Irresistible' to Profit-Driven Media." Retrieved June 30, 2000 from http://www.fair.org/extra/0005/thornhill.html.
17. Ibid.
18. Steven Pinker, *The Blank Slate: The Modern Denial of Human Nature* (New York: Viking, 2002), 371, defends Thornhill and Palmer's telling women to dress differently as a form of rape prevention on the grounds that we don't live in a utopia. However, Pinker also notes that chemical castration drastically reduces the recidivism rate for rapists, but nevertheless makes clear that he does not advocate chemical castration because such would raise constitutional issues about privacy and punishment. Pinker's willingness to sacrifice women's freedom in order to reduce the rape rate, but not men's, is somewhat incongruous.
19. Greg Gutfeld, "The Mysteries of Sex … Explained!," *Men's Health*, April 1999, 76.
20. Ibid.
21. Robert Wright, *The Moral Animal: Evolutionary Psychology and Everyday Life* (New York: Pantheon, 1994), 45.
22. Ibid., 50.
23. Ibid., 52.
24. David M. Buss, *The Evolution of Desire: Strategies of Human Mating* (New York: Basic Books, 1994).
25. ABC News, *Day One*, 1995.
26. Ibid.
27. Geoffrey Cowley, "The Biology of Beauty: What Science Has Discovered About Sex Appeal," *Newsweek* 127 (1996): 62, 64.
28. Ibid., 66.
29. Ibid.
30. Ronnie Godeanu, prod. *The Nature of Sex: Sex and the Human Animal* (Guildfordx, England: Genesis Productions, 1993).
31. Clive Bromhall, dir., "Beyond Survival" (episode), *Desmond Morris' The Human Animal: A Personal View of the Human Species.* (New York: Discovery Communications, 1999). See also Desmond Morris, *The Naked Ape: A Zoologist's Study of the Human Animal* (1967; reprint New York: Dell, 1999).
32. Annaud, *Quest for Fire.*
33. Fred Schepisi, dir., *Iceman,* (Los Angeles: Universal Pictures, 1984).
34. Les Mayfield, dir., *Encino Man* (Hollywood, CA: Hollywood Pictures, 1992).
35. Cheryl B. Travis, "Talking Evolution and Selling Difference," in *Evolution, Gender, and Rape*, ed. Cheryl B. Travis (Cambridge, MA: MIT Press, 2003), 11.
36. Craig Hagstrom, *The Passionate Ape: Bad Sex, Strong Love, and Human Evolution* (Bainbridge Island, WA: RiverForest Press, 2001), 11.

37. See Annalee Newitz, "My Darling, My Darwin," *San Francisco Bay Guardian*, January 31, 2001, "Techsploitation;" retrieved February 22, 2007, from http://www.techsploitation.com; and Craig Hagstrom, "Passionate Ape;" retrieved February 22, 2007 from http://www.passionateape.com.
38. See http://www.passionateape.com/links.htm.
39. Hagstrom, *The Passionate Ape,* 338.
40. Ibid., 340.
41. Ibid., 343.
42. Ibid., 372.
43. Jeff Hood, *The Silverback Gorilla Syndrome: Transforming Primitive Man* (Santa Fe, NM: Adventures in Spirit, 1999), 1.
44. Ibid., 4.
45. Ibid., 57–63.
46. See W. Bradford Wilcox, Soft Patriarchs, *New Men: How Christianity Fathers and Husbands* (Chicago: University of Chicago Press, 2004).
47. Pierre Bourdieu, *Distinction: A Social Critique of the Judgment of Taste* (Cambridge, MA: Harvard University Press, 1984).
48. Pierre Bourdieu, *The Logic of Practice*, trans. Richard Nice (Sanford, CA: Sanford University Press, 1990).
49. Pierre Bourdieu, *Masculine Domination*, trans. Richard Nice (Stanford, CA: Sanford University Press, 2001).
50. Richard Widick, "Flesh and the Free Market (On Taking Bourdieu to the Options Exchange)," *Theory and Society* 32 (2003): 716.
51. Ibid., 701.
52. Ibid.
53. Bourdieu, *Masculine Domination*, 39.
54. Ibid., 113.
55. Steph Lawler, "Rules of Engagement: Habitus, Power and Resistance," in *Feminism After Bourdieu*, eds. Lisa Adkins and Bev Skeggs (Oxford: Blackwell, 2004), 112–13.
56. Lois McNay, "Agency and Experience: Gender As a Lived Relation," in *Feminism After Bourdieu*, eds. Lisa Adkins and Bev Skeggs (Oxford: Blackwell, 2004), 177.
57. See McNay, "Agency and Experience," 175–90, for a discussion of emotional compensation and lived experience.
58. See Beverley Skeggs, *Formations of Class and Gender: Becoming Respectable* (London: Sage, 1997), for a study pointing this out about working-class women.
59. R. W. Connell, *Gender and Power: Society, the Person and Sexual Politics* (Cambridge, U.K.: Polity, 1987), 84.
60. Ibid., 85.
61. Thomas F. Gieryn, *Cultural Boundaries of Science: Credibility on the Line* (Chicago: University of Chicago Press, 1999), 1.
62. Paul Rabinow, *Making PCR, A Story of Biotechnology* (Chicago: University of Chicago Press, 1996), 101–2.
63. Ibid., 102.

Chapter 4

1. See Kevin T. Berrill and Gregory M. Herek, eds., *Hate Crimes: Confronting Violence against Lesbians and Gay Men* (Newbury Park, CA: Sage, 1992); and Gregory M. Herek, "On Heterosexual Masculinity: Some Psychical Consequences of the Social Construction of Gender and Sexuality," *American Behavioral Scientist* 29, no. 5 (1986): 563–7, on how ideas of natural manhood perpetuate queer bashing, and Stoltenberg, *Refusing to Be a Man,* on how ideas of natural manhood perpetuate rape.
2. See Barbara Herrnstein Smith, *Contingencies of Value: Alternative Perspectives for Critical Theory* (Cambridge, MA: Harvard University Press, 1988).

3. It should be noted, though, that evolutionary theorists themselves are, by and large, more socially and politically liberal than, say, the Catholic Church. Edward O. Wilson, *On Human Nature* (Cambridge, MA: Harvard University Press, 1987), 141, states that the natural law theory of the Catholic Church wrongly assumes that the biological significance of sex is the insemination of wives by husbands. As I discuss later, Wilson claims that the biological function of sexual pleasure in human beings is not insemination, but bonding. Thus, to a large extent, it is the cultural context in which these matters get taken up that make evolutionary theories into secular extensions of Judeo–Christian heterosexism.

4. Steven Seidman, *Romantic Longings: Love in America, 1830–1980* (New York: Routledge, 1991), 181.

5. See, for example, Donna Haraway, *Primate Visions: Gender, Race and Nature in the World of Modern Science* (New York: Routledge, 1989); Helen E. Longino, *Science as Social Knowledge: Values and Objectivity in Scientific Inquiry* (Princeton: Princeton University Press, 1991); Sandra Harding and Merrill B. Hintikka, eds., *Discovering Reality* (Dordrecht, The Netherlands: D. Reidel, 1983); and Nancy Tuana, ed., *Feminism and Science*, Bloomington: Indiana University Press, 1989).

6. See, for example, Alexander Doty, *Making Things Perfectly Queer: Interpreting Mass Culture* (Minneapolis: University of Minnesota Press, 1993); Michael Warner, "Fear of a Queer Planet," *Social Text* 29 (1991): 3–17; and the essays in the "Queer Theory" issue of *differences* 3, no. 2 (1991).

7. For more examples of the sexual politics of scientific stories, see Haraway, *Primate Visions*, on primate stories; Longino, *Science as Social Knowledge*, on sex differences research; and Emily Martin, "The Egg and the Sperm: How Science Has Constructed a Romance Based on Stereotypical Male-Female Roles," *Signs: Journal of Women in Culture and Society* 16, no. 3 (1991): 485-501, on egg and sperm stories.

8. David P. Barash, "Sexual Selection in Birdland," *Psychology Today*, March 1978, 82–86); David P. Barash, "The Sociobiology of Rape in Mallards (*Anas platyrhynchos*): Responses of the Mated Male," *Science* 197, no. 4305 (1977): 788–89.

9. Scott Morris, "Darwin and the Double Standard," *Playboy*, May 1983, 109.

10. Ibid., 110.

11. Ibid., 111; emphasis in the original.

12. Christine Gorman, "Sizing Up the Sexes," *Time*, January 20, 1992, 48.

13. Ibid.

14. I do not wish to imply, with the filter imagery, that there is an objective lens behind the filter. Uncommonly held assumptions, such as feminist or queer meanings of gender and sexuality, are also conceptual filters through which scientific evidence is interpreted.

15. Gorman, "Sizing Up the Sexes," 45.

16. Ibid.

17. See Longino, *Science as Social Knowledge*.

18. Clive Bromhall, dir., "Beyond Survival" (episode), *Desmond Morris' The Human Animal: A Personal View of the Human Species*. (New York: Discovery Communications, 1999).

19. See Jared Diamond, *Why Is Sex Fun? The Evolution of Human Sexuality* (New York: Basic Books, 1997).

20. Ibid., 144.

21. Ibid., 144–45.

22. Ibid., 145.

23. Ibid.

24. Robin Baker, *Sperm Wars: Infidelity, Sexual Conflict, and Other Bedroom Battles* (New York: Thunder's Mouth, 2006).

25. Ibid., 283.

26. It is worth noting that, to introduce the issue of bisexuality, Baker, *Sperm Wars*, 276–82, offers an explicit scenario in which a man molests his nephew; the nephew enjoys the homosexual sex and becomes a bisexual in his adult life, cheating on his various partners with both men and women. This characterization wrongly presents the sexual assault of children as something boys enjoy, as if this is how men become gay or bisexual, and that bisexuals must be promiscuous cheaters. It also contributes to the homophobic stereotype that gay men are dangerous child molesters. Baker certainly presents scenarios in which heterosexuals lie and cheat in sexual relationships; but he also presents far more scenes of heterosexual sex, leaving the reader with a more evenhanded view of what heterosexuals do.

27. Michael V. Studd and Urs E. Gattiker, "The Evolutionary Psychology of Sexual Harassment in Organizations," *Ethology and Sociobiology* 12, no. 4 (1991): 249–290, 287.

28. Ibid.

29. Ibid.

30. Ibid.

31. Ibid.

32. Catharine A. MacKinnon, *Sexual Harassment of Working Women: A Case of Sex Discrimination* (New Haven, CT: Yale University Press, 1979).

33. The fact that offices and other modern workplaces did not exist in the EEA might mean, for evolutionary theorists, that coercive male sexual behavior in the EEA did result in reproductive success, whether or not it does today. However, these theorists use the modern workplace as evidence that coercive sexual behavior was rewarded (in terms of reproductive success) in the EEA. I am suggesting that what goes on in the modern workplace could be taken as evidence for a different hypothesis about the behavior that was rewarded in the EEA.

34. Studd and Gattiker, "Evolutionary Psychology," 284; emphasis in the original.

35. Mary Ellen Strote, "Man the Visual Animal," *Muscle and Fitness*, February 1994, 168, quoting Donald Symons, *The Evolution of Human Sexuality* (New York: Oxford University Press, 1979).

36. Strote, "Man the Visual Animal," 168.

37. See David M. Buss, *The Evolution of Desire: Strategies of Human Mating* (New York: Basic Books, 1994).

38. That men do not universally find visibly pregnant women unattractive, even though copulating with them is a guaranteed reproductive dead end, is evidence against the theory that men have evolved with particularly keen abilities to distinguish between, through differential sexual attraction to, fertile and infertile bodies.

39. Donald Symons furnished this useful observation about sugar in his 1989 seminar on human nature at the University of California–Santa Barbara.

40. See David Barash, "Why Sugar is Sweet," in *The Whisperings Within: Evolution and the Origin of Human Nature* (New York: Harper and Row, 1979), 16–45.

41. David P. Barash, "Sexual Selection in Birdland," *Psychology Today*, March 1978, 84.

42. See Barash, "Sociobiology;" and Barash, "Sexual Selection."

43. Ibid.

44. Stephen J. Gould, *The Panda's Thumb: More Reflections in Natural History* (New York: Norton, 1980), 20.

45. Edward O. Wilson, *On Human Nature* (Cambridge, MA: Harvard University Press, 1987), 144–45.

46. See William B. Rubinstein, ed., *Lesbians, Gay Men, and the Law* (New York: New Press, 1993).

47. Buss, *The Evolution of Desire*, 60.

48. Symons, *The Evolution of Human Sexuality*, 304; emphasis added.

49. Buss, *The Evolution of Desire*, 61.

50. See Eve Kosofsky Sedgwick, *Epistemology of the Closet* (Berkeley and Los Angeles: University of California Press, 1990).

51. Ibid.

52. I do not mean to imply that no scholar has ever argued that humans might be bisexual. Certainly Sigmund Freud and others are well known for just such an assertion (although they did not base their arguments on now current versions of evolutionary theory). My point is that evolutionary theorists have not entertained bisexuality as a hypothesis for which to provide evolutionary evidence, even though nothing about the theory of evolution automatically implies a heterosexual human nature in any individual or in the majority of humans. My interest in evolutionary theory, then, is not that it is the one theory that holds the promise of positing humans as bisexual, but that it has so consistently been used in recent years to undermine bisexual hypotheses, replacing them with one of innate male heterosexual predation.

53. This could be because copulation need not be pleasurable to be adaptive. Recall our poor beheaded male praying mantis; his decapitation could not have been selected against if the copulation usually resulted in a fertilization. In any case, evolutionary theorists have not offered a story in which our foresisters bonded sexually together.

54. Wilson, *On Human Nature*, 142.

55. Ibid., 141-42.

56. Ibid., 144–45.

57. Given Wilson's reputation as conservative among some academics, it is worth noting that his claims do not dismiss homosexuals as evolutionary misfits or dysfunctional perverts. For instance, in *On Human Nature,* he suggests that homosexual men in some of the "more primitive cultures" often became shamans, peacemakers, and advisors to tribal leaders, and in Western society score higher than heterosexuals on intelligence tests, select white collar professions disproportionately, are generally well adapted in social relationships, and often enter careers in which they deal directly with other people (146). He also remarks that it would be both unfortunate and illogical to make past genetic adaptedness a necessary criterion for current acceptance (147).

58. Roz Chast, "Scientists Discover the Gene for Heterosexuality in Men" (cartoon), *New Yorker*, August 2, 1993. Available to view online at www.cartoonbank.com.

59. See Judith Butler, *Gender Trouble: Feminism and the Subversion of Identity* (New York: Routledge, 1990); Andrea Dworkin, *Woman Hating* (New York: E. P. Dutton, 1974); and Adrienne Rich, "Compulsory Heterosexuality and Lesbian Existence," *Signs* 5, no. 4 (1980): 631–60.

60. See Jeffrey Weeks, *Sex, Politics, and Society: The Regulation of Sexuality Since 1800* (New York: Longman, 1981).

61. Simon LeVay, "A Difference in Hypothalamic Structure between Heterosexual and Homosexual Men," *Science* 253, no. 5023 (1991): 1034–37, is one of several recent studies that have been reported in the media. See also J. Michael Bailey and Richard C. Pillard, "A Genetic Study of Male Sexual Orientation," *Archives of General Psychiatry* 48 (1991): 1089–96; and Dean Hamer and Peter Copeland, *The Science of Desire: The Search for the Gay Gene and the Biology of Behavior* (New York: Simon and Schuster, 1994). My concern here is not to review or critique all of these studies, but to point to the ways in which studies that search for a biological substratum for homosexual orientation, desire, or identity reify a sex binarism, which is, paradoxically, part and parcel of heterosexism.

62. Gorman, "Sizing Up the Sexes," 45; LeVay, "Hypothalamic Structure."

63. Gorman, "Sizing Up the Sexes," 48.

64. S. Begley and D. Gelman, "What Causes People to Be Homosexual?" *Newsweek* 118, no. 11 (1991): 52.

65. Another example of the press extending and twisting the modest message of a scientific study is the *National Inquirer's* report of Hamer's research, which suggests a link between DNA markers on the X chromosome and male sexual orientation. The *Inquirer's* headline read, "Simple Injection Will Let Gay Men Turn Straight, Doctors Report," according to Hamer and Copeland, *The Science of Desire*, 18.

66. Sedgwick, *Epistemology*, 8.

67. See Butler, *Gender Trouble*; and Sedgwick, *Epistemology*.

68. The conflation of sexual activity/penetration/agency and heterosexual manhood/ masculinity may account for the frequency with which scientific studies focus on explaining men's sexuality and not women's (in addition to the reasons already mentioned in note 1, above). In our cultural logic, it is more difficult to imagine women as active, desiring sexual subjects whose genetic or biochemical structure explains the direction of their amorous attentions. The construction of men as first-class citizens who are active sexual agents, and the construction of penetration as an act by which a first-class citizen establishes himself as superior to the person being penetrated, means that getting penetrated makes one a woman/fag/second-class citizen/ degraded. Here it should be obvious how sexism and heterosexism work together through the meaning of penetration. To penetrate means, culturally, to degrade— for men and women—but is thought to be appropriate to do to women, since they lack the entitlement to first-class citizenship status. If a man wants to be penetrated, or wants to penetrate someone socially deemed impenetrable (i.e., another man), he threatens the order by which male privilege is defined and legitimated. For discussions of these issues, see Leo Bersani, "Is the Rectum a Grave?" *October* 43 (1987): 197–222; and David M. Halperin, "One Hundred Years of Homosexuality," in *One Hundred Years of Homosexuality and Other Essays on Greek Love* (New York: Routledge, 1990), 30–33.

69. Halperin, "One Hundred Years of Homosexuality," 27.

70. Hamer and Copeland, *The Science of Desire*, 65, remarks that their search for the "gay gene" accounted for an individual who may have, say, identified as heterosexual until the age of 21 and then came out as gay. Their research presumes that a man might change his sexual behavior but not his sexual orientation.

71. See Halperin, "One Hundred Years of Homosexuality;" Sedgwick, *Epistemology*.

72. See Tomás Almaguer, "Chicano Men: A Cartography of Homosexual Identity and Behavior," *differences* 3, no. 2 (1991): 75–100.

73. See Edward Stein, "The Relevance of Scientific Research about Sexual Orientation to Lesbian and Gay Rights," *Journal of Homosexuality* 27, nos. 3–4 (1994): 269–308, for a more detailed argument that scientific research on sexual orientation is irrelevant for advancing the moral and civic entitlement of gay men and lesbians. Dean Hamer, of the "gay gene" study, was dismayed when the father of two gay sons wrote him to say that Hamer's work that said homosexuality might be genetic finally allowed him to forgive himself for having gay sons. Hamer and Copeland, *The Science of Desire*, 19, explain that he decided to forgive his sons because we found a genetic link to homosexuality. But what if the experiment had failed? Or what if we gave his family a blood test and found they didn't have the 'gay gene,' that the sons were gay for some other reason? Then would this father go back to blaming himself for raising two gay sons, and would they be less worthy of his love?

74. Certainly gay-rights lawyers have tried to use, or appeal to, foundationalist logic in courts, hoping to secure gay rights by presenting evidence for the naturalness of homosexuality. I do not have space in this essay to debate the pros and cons of foundationalism; but, see Janet Halley, "Sexual Orientation and the Politics of Biology: A Critique of the Argument from Immutibility," *Stanford Law Review* 46, no. 3 (1994): 503–68, for a discussion of the legal strategy; and Smith, *Contingencies of Value*, for a discussion of the problems with foundationalism.

75. These stories deal with femininity relatively infrequently. However, the construction of man as heterosexual predator positions woman as the naturally passive other in this heterosexual equation.

76. Steven Seidman, *Difference Troubles: Queering Social Theory and Sexual Politics* (Cambridge, U.K.: Cambridge University Press, 1997), xi.

77. See Wendy Brown, "Feminist Hesitations, Postmodern Exposures," *differences* 3, no. 1 (1991): 63–84; and Smith, *Contingencies of Value*.

78. See Stephen Jay Gould, *The Panda's Thumb: More Reflections in Natural History* (New York: W. W. Norton, 1980).
79. Patricia A. Gowaty, "Sexual Terms in Sociobiology: Emotionally Evocative and Paradoxically, Jargon," *Animal Behavior* 30 (1982): 630–31.
80. See George C. Williams, "Huxley's Evolution and Ethics in Sociobiological Perspective," *Zygon* 23, no. 4 (1988): 383–407.
81. See Sarah Franklin, "Essentialism, Which Essentialism? Some Implications of Reproductive and Genetic Techno-Science," *Journal of Homosexuality* 24, nos. 3–4 (1993): 27–39, for a discussion of the way the AIDS epidemic and new reproductive technologies could have disrupted the "natural" basis for the nuclear family and heterosexual privilege, but instead reconsolidated it.

Chapter 5

1. See, for example, Charles Pickstone, *The Divinity of Sex: The Search for Ecstasy in a Secular Age* (New York: St. Martin's, 1996).
2. Steven Seidman, *Difference Troubles: Queering Social Theory and Sexual Politics* (Cambridge, U.K.: Cambridge University Press, 1997), 229.
3. Charles J. Lumsden and Edward O. Wilson, *Genes, Mind and Culture: The Coevolutionary Process* (Cambridge, MA: Harvard University Press, 1981), 179.
4. Charles J. Lumsden and Edward O. Wilson, *Promethean Fire: Reflections on the Origin of Mind* (Cambridge, MA: Harvard University Press, 1983).
5. See Steven E. Rhoads, *Taking Sex Differences Seriously* (San Francisco: Encounter Books, 2004).
6. See David M. Buss, *The Evolution of Desire: Strategies of Human Mating* (New York: Basic Books, 1994).
7. See David M. Buss, "Sex Differences in Human Mate Preferences: Evolutionary Hypotheses Tested in 37 Cultures," *Behavioral and Brain Sciences* 12 (1989): 1–49.
8. See David M. Buss, Abbott, M., Angleitner, A., Asherian, A., Biaggio, A., Blanco-VillaSeñor, A., Bruchon-Schweitzer, M., Ch'u, Hai-yuan, Czapinski, J., DeRaad, B., Ekehammar, B., Fioravanti, M., Georgas, J., Gjerde, P., Guttman, R., Hazan, F., Iwawaki, S., Janakiramaiah, N., Khosroshani, F., Kreitler, S., Lachenicht, L., Lee, M., Liik, K., Little, B., Lohamy, N., Makim, S., Mika, S., Moadel-Shahid, M., Moane, G., Montero, M., Mundy-Castle, A.C., Niit, T., Nsenduluka, E., Peltzer, K., Pienkowski, R., Pirttila-Backman, A., Ponce De Leon, J., Rousseau, J., Runco, M.A., Safir, M.P., Samuels, C., Sanitioso, R., Schweitzer, B., Serpell, R., Smid, N., Spencer, C., Tadinac, M., Todorova, E.N., Troland, K., Van den Brande, L., Van Heck, G., Van Langenhove, L., and Yang, K., "International Preferences in Selecting Mates: A Study of 37 Cultures," *Journal of Cross-Cultural Psychology* 21 (1990): 5–47.
9. Ibid., 42–44.
10. See Edward O. Wilson, *Sociobiology: The New Synthesis*, 25th anniversary ed. (Cambridge, MA: Belknap Press of Harvard University Press, 2000); and Stephen J. Gould, *Ever Since Darwin: Reflections in Natural History* (New York: W. W. Norton, 1977).
11. Gould, *Ever Since Darwin*, 254–57.
12. See Richard Alexander, *Darwinism and Human Affairs* (Seattle: University of Washington Press, 1979).
13. See Robin Baker, *Sperm Wars: Infidelity, Sexual Conflict, and Other Bedroom Battles* (New York: Thunder's Mouth, 2006).
14. Ibid., xx.
15. Ibid., xvii.
16. Ibid., 374.
17. David P. Barash and Eve Lipton, *Making Sense of Sex: How Genes and Gender Influence Our Relationships* (Washington: Island Press, 1997), 212.

18. Ibid., 209.
19. F. Roes, "An Interview with Richard Dawkins," Human Ethology Bulletin 12, no. 1 (1997): 1–3. Quoted in Ullica Segerstråle, *Defenders of the Truth: The Battle for Science in the Sociobiology Debate and Beyond* (Oxford: Oxford University Press, 2000), 374.
20. Malcolm Potts and Roger Short, *Ever Since Adam and Eve: The Evolution of Human Sexuality* (New York: Cambridge University Press, 1999), 326.
21. Steven Pinker, *The Blank Slate: The Modern Denial of Human Nature* (New York: Viking, 2002).
22. Ibid.; see also Steve Fuller, *The New Sociological Imagination* (London: Sage, 2006).
23. See Bernice L. Hausman, "Do Boys Have to Be Boys?: Gender, Narrativity, and the John/Joan Case," *NWSA Journal* 12, no. 3 (2000): 114–38, for an excellent analysis of the complexities of what made Joan still feel like, and ultimately opt to change surgically back to, John.
24. Pinker, *The Blank Slate*, 343.
25. Ibid., 337.
26. Marlene Zuk, *Sexual Selections: What We Can and Can't Learn about Sex from Animals* (Berkeley and Los Angeles: University of California Press, 2002), 4.
27. Ibid., 16.
28. John Michael, *Anxious Intellects: Academic Professionals, Public Intellectuals, and Enlightenment Values* (Durham, NC: Duke University Press, 2000), 170.
29. Ibid.
30. Henry Bauer, "Antiscience in Current Science and Technology Studies" in *Beyond the Science Wars: The Missing Discourse about Science and Society*, ed. Ullica Segerstråle (Albany: State University of New York Press, 2000), 49–50.
31. Ullica Segerstråle, *Defenders of the Truth: The Battle for Science in the Sociobiology Debate and Beyond* (Oxford, U.K.: Oxford University Press, 2000).
32. Paul R. Gross and Norman Levitt, *Higher Superstition: The Academic Left and Its Quarrels with Science* (Baltimore: John Hopkins University Press, 1994).
33. Segerstråle, *Defenders*, 344.
34. See Donna Haraway, *Primate Visions: Gender, Race and Nature in the World of Modern Science* (New York: Routledge, 1989). However, Haraway is mentioned only once, regarding a different issue, in Segerstråle, *Defenders*.
35. For detailed arguments about value-laden science that does not reject the importance of scientific study, see Donna Haraway, *Modest-Witness@Second Millennium. FemaleMan-Meets-OncoMouse: Feminism and Technoscience* (New York: Routledge, 1997); and Helen E. Longino, *Science as Social Knowledge: Values and Objectivity in Scientific Inquiry* (Princeton, NJ: Princeton University Press, 1991).
36. Paul R. Gross, "Bashful Eggs, Macho Sperm, and Tonypandy," in *A House Built on Sand: Exposing Postmodernist Myths about Science*, ed. Noretta Koertge (New York: Oxford University Press, 1998), 59–70.
37. Noretta Koertge, ed., *A House Built on Sand: Exposing Postmodernist Myths about Science* (New York: Oxford University Press, 1998).
38. Steve Fuller, "Science Studies Through the Looking Glass: An Intellectual Itinerary," in *Beyond the Science Wars: The Missing Discourse about Science and Society*, ed. Ullica Segerstråle (Albany: State University of New York Press, 2000), 207.
39. Michael, *Anxious Intellects*, 151–53.
40. Ibid., 153.
41. Segerstråle, *Defenders*. The essays in the collection by Cheryl B. Travis, ed., *Evolution, Gender, and Rape* (Cambridge, MA: MIT Press, 2003), which responds to Randy Thornhill and Craig T. Palmer, *A Natural History of Rape: Biological Bases of Sexual Coercion* (Cambridge, MA: MIT Press, 2000), exemplify some of that type of attack, as authors angrily nag scientists to change.
42. Clifford Geertz, "A Lab of One's Own: Feminism and Science," *New York Review of Books* 37, no. 17 (1990): 105–7.

43. See Anthony Giddens, *Transformation of Intimacy: Sexuality, Love and Eroticism in Modern Societies* (Stanford, CA: Stanford University Press, 1992).

44. Susan Faludi, *Stiffed: The Betrayal of the American Man* (New York: HarperCollins, 1999), 607.

45. See Barbara Ehrenreich, "The Decline of Patriarchy," in *Constructing Masculinity*, eds. Maurice Berger, Brian Wallis, and Simon Watson (New York: Routledge, 1995), 284-290.

46. Michael S. Kimmel, *Manhood in America: A Cultural History* (New York: Free Press, 1996).

47. For a similar argument about the appeal of pornographic fantasies in the context of men's slipping privilege, see Michael S. Kimmel, *The Gender of Desire: Essays on Male Sexuality* (Albany: State University of New York Press, 2005), 91–95.

48. See George F. Gilder, *Sexual Suicide* (New York: Quadrangle, 1973); George F. Gilder, *Naked Nomads: Unmarried Men in America* (New York: Quadrangle, 1974); Steven Goldberg, *The Inevitability of Patriarchy* (New York: Morrow, 1973); and Norman Mailer, *The Prisoner of Sex* (Boston: Little, Brown, 1971).

49. Kimmel, *Manhood*, 274.

50. Giddens, *Transformation of Intimacy*, 178.

51. Seidman, *Difference Troubles*, 227–29.

52. Giddens, *Transformation of Intimacy*, 203.

53. Ibid., 116–17.

54. Kimmel, *The Gender of Desire*, 127–37.

55. Ibid.

56. Ibid., 137.

57. Ibid., 232–34.

58. Kimmel, *Manhood in America*, 335.

59. Ibid., 333.

60. Giddens, *Transformation of Intimacy*, 117.

61. Kimmel, *Manhood in America*, 290.

62. Ibid., 326.

63. My colleague Jammie Price offered this insight, describing the logic as one of medicalization. As she put it, a man might medicate his inner gorilla as well.

64. See William Bradford Wilcox, *Soft Patriarchs, New Men: How Christianity Shapes Fathers and Husbands* (Chicago: University of Chicago Press, 2004).

65. Wilcox, *Soft Patriarchs*, 9, acknowledges borrowing the term "patriarchal bargain" from Connie Anderson and Michael A. Messner, whose 1997 conference paper used the term.

66. Giddens, *Transformation of Intimacy*, 146.

67. Ibid., 130.

68. Will Wright, *Wild Knowledge: Science, Language, and Social Life in a Fragile Environment* (Minneapolis: University of Minnesota Press, 1992), makes this argument about ecology and knowledge.

69. Seidman, *Difference Troubles*, 93.

70. See José Esteban Muñoz, *Disidentifications: Queers of Color and the Performance of Politics* (Minneapolis: University of Minnesota Press, 1999).

71. It's possible that, even after embracing identity as socially constructed, some men might adopt a caveman ruggedness as a self-consciously fictional identity or pastiche personality. I'm not saying men shouldn't have fun, and don't wish to sound like Jerry Falwell or Tipper Gore, who tell men to stop being "bad boys." If guys want to watch violent cop movies, listen to violent music lyrics, and pretend they're cavemen, that's fine with me. I only hope they do so with the appropriate sense of humor.

72. Patricia Clough, *Feminist Thought: Desire, Power, and Academic Discourse.* (Cambridge, MA: Blackwell, 1994), 122.

INDEX